TOP 10
TOKYO

Top 10 Tokyo Highlights

The Top 10 of Everything

CONTENTS

Tokyo Area by Area

Streetsmart

Within each Top 10 list in this book, no hierarchy of quality or popularity is implied. All 10 are, in the editor's opinion, of roughly equal merit. Throughout this book, floors are referred to in accordance with American usage, i.e., the first floor is at ground level.

Title page, front cover and spine *Senso-ji Temple in Asakusa*
Back cover, clockwise from top left *Cherry trees line Meguro River; Tokyo skyline with Rainbow Bridge and the iconic Tokyo Tower; Sushi rolls served with tea; Senso-ji Temple; Busy crossing in Shinjuku*

Welcome to
Tokyo

Everything that is both traditional and modern about Japan is found in Tokyo. It's a city of amazing architecture and fashion, delicious cuisine, and cutting-edge technology. Artistic and cultural traditions have been honed to perfection but the city is also a master of innovation and reinvention. With Eyewitness Top 10 Tokyo, it's yours to explore.

You may have in mind the Tokyo of popular imagination, a perpetually buzzing, utterly contemporary metropolis, illuminated by neon. But this is also a city of tranquil gardens, ancient temples, and shrines, such as the **Koishikawa Korakuen Garden** and **Meiji Shrine**. Prepare to be beguiled by the beauty of traditional arts and crafts available to view in museums or buy in stores that have been tended by the same families for generations.

And then there is the food. The famous fish market may have moved to a new location in Toyosu but many specialist food stores remain in the Tsukiji area, an ideal introduction to Japan's unique culinary culture. The tastes of Edo – the old name for the capital – linger in the backstreets of **Yanaka** and the precincts of **Asakusa**. Best of all, despite its sprawling size and millions of inhabitants, Tokyo works like a dream. Public transportation is fast, efficient, and inexpensive. Polite service is a given, as are clean streets that are safe to walk any time of the day or night.

Whether you're visiting for a weekend or a week, our Top 10 guide brings together the best of everything the city has to offer, from the glitz of **Ginza** to the street fashion of **Shibuya**. The guide has useful tips throughout, from seeking out what's free to avoiding the crowds, plus nine easy-to-follow itineraries designed to tie together a clutch of sights in a short space of time. Add inspiring photography and detailed maps, and you've got the essential pocket-sized travel companion. **Enjoy the book, and enjoy Tokyo.**

Clockwise from top: **Senso-ji Temple**; exhibit, **Kite Museum**; **National Art Center**; skyline with **Mt Fuji** behind; **Daibutsu Buddha, Kamakura**; **Kabukicho district**; **Chidorigafuchi moat, Imperial Palace**

Exploring Tokyo

Don't be fazed by Tokyo's crowds and hyperactivity. The following itineraries include the very best sights in this fascinating, multi-layered city. There's also time for shopping, relaxing, and savoring Tokyo's delicious culinary scene.

The Edo-Tokyo Museum has fabulous displays.

The interior of Senso-ji Temple is just as beautiful as its exterior.

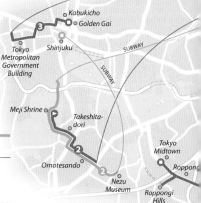

Two Days in Tokyo

Day ❶
MORNING
Take a crash course in art and culture at **Tokyo National Museum** (see pp24–7). Then, stroll around **Ueno Park** (see pp20–21) and the bustling **Ameyoko Market** (see p67).

AFTERNOON
Explore the **Edo-Tokyo Museum** (see pp18–19) before enjoying a bird's-eye view of the city from **Tokyo Skytree** (see p89). Meander through Asakusa and the grounds of the **Senso-ji Temple** (see pp14–15). Board the water bus and cruise down the **Sumida River** (see pp16–17). Afterwards, catch a show at **Kabukiza Theatre** (see p81).

Day ❷
MORNING
Discover the moats, stone walls, and gardens of the **Imperial Palace** (see pp12–13). Then, take in the excellent collection at the **National Museum of Modern Art** (see p12) and the **Crafts Gallery** (see p13).

AFTERNOON
Crunch down the gravel pathway to **Meiji Shrine** (see pp30–31), and then go shopping on Harajuku's **Takeshita-dori** (see p56) and tree-lined **Omotesando** (see p101). The nearby **Nezu Museum** (see p100) has a serene garden with a teahouse. In the evening, enjoy the electric vibe of **Shinjuku** (see pp106–11).

Four Days in Tokyo

Day ❶
MORNING
Have breakfast in **Tsukiji Outer Market** (see p66), then tour the **Hama Rikyu Garden** (see p82). View the old wooden gates fronting **Zojo-ji Temple** (see p97) with **Tokyo Tower** (see p96), an icon of the city, in the background.

AFTERNOON
Enjoy the galleries and museums of Roppongi and then browse the shops of **Roppongi Hills** (see p94) and **Tokyo Midtown** (see p95), where there are also great places to eat and drink.

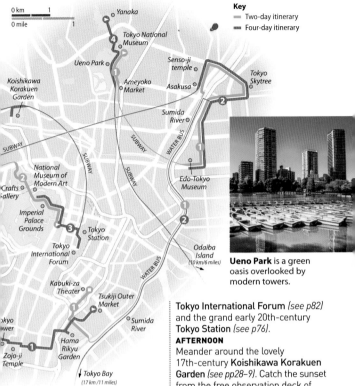

Key
— Two-day itinerary
— Four-day itinerary

0 km 1
0 mile 1

Yanaka

Tokyo National Museum

Ueno Park

Koishikawa Korakuen Garden

Ameyoko Market

Senso-ji temple

Asakusa

Tokyo Skytree

Sumida River

National Museum of Modern Art

Crafts Gallery

SUBWAY

Imperial Palace Grounds

Tokyo Station

Tokyo International Forum

Edo-Tokyo Museum

Kabuki-za Theater

Tsukiji Outer Market

Odaiba Island (10 km/6 miles)

WATER BUS

Tokyo Tower

Sumida River

Hama Rikyu Garden

Zojo-ji Temple

Tokyo Bay (17 km/11 miles)

Ueno Park is a green oasis overlooked by modern towers.

Day ❷
MORNING
Pay your respects at **Meiji Shrine** (see pp30–31), and then browse quirky styles on **Takeshita-dori** (see p56) and high fashion along **Omotesando** (see p101). Cross town for lunch in Asakusa and to view the sights around **Senso-ji** (see pp14–15).
AFTERNOON
Ascend **Tokyo Skytree** (see p89), learn about the city's history at the **Edo-Tokyo Museum** (see pp18–19), and sail into Tokyo Bay on a cruise down the **Sumida River** (see pp16–17).

Day ❸
MORNING
Tour the grounds of the **Imperial Palace** (see pp12–13) and then visit the Marunouchi district, home to the contemporary architecture of the

Tokyo International Forum (see p82) and the grand early 20th-century **Tokyo Station** (see p76).
AFTERNOON
Meander around the lovely 17th-century **Koishikawa Korakuen Garden** (see pp28–9). Catch the sunset from the free observation deck of **Tokyo Metropolitan Government Building** (see p109) in Shinjuku, and then hit the **Kabukicho** (see p106) entertainment area and the warren of drinking dens in **Golden Gai** (see p107).

Day ❹
MORNING
Get acquainted with the shrines, temples, and traditional stores of **Yanaka** (see pp32–3). Afterwards, check out the collection at the **Tokyo National Museum** (see pp24–7) and stroll around **Ueno Park** (see pp20–21).
AFTERNOON
Ride the train to **Odaiba Island** (see pp34–5) to marvel at robot technology at the fascinating **National Museum of Emerging Science and Innovation** (see p35). Finish your day at the extraordinary bathhouse **Oedo Onsen Monogatari** (see p34).

Top 10 Tokyo Highlights

Detail on the elaborate exterior of the main hall, Senso-ji Temple

Tokyo Highlights

The easternmost of the great Asian cities, Tokyo is a city of perpetual change and one that embraces transformation. More interested in the future than the past, it nevertheless carries its history and traditions into the present. This intensely cultural capital is one of the world's most energetic and creative cities. The following 10 sights are a must for any first-time visitor, but there is always something new to discover.

Imperial Palace Grounds

Part Forbidden City, part public park, the palace grounds are encircled by moats, stone walls, ancient bridges, keeps, and gardens – elements in the history of the original city (see pp12–13).

Senso-ji Temple

The grounds of this temple are packed with attractions, beginning at Kaminari-mon ("Thunder Gate") and the commercial corridor of Nakamise-dori (see pp14–15).

Sumida River

An excursion starting under its famous bridges is a journey through the history and development of the city (see pp16–17).

Edo-Tokyo Museum

Blending history, art, and architecture, this stunning museum traces the history of the city from Edo Castle to the 1964 Tokyo Olympics (see pp18–19).

Ueno Park

A compendium of Japanese cultural history, this park contains mausoleums, temples, museums, a zoo, and a lotus pond. With 1,000 cherry trees, the park is at its best when blossoms are out in spring (see pp20–21).

Tokyo National Museum
The world's largest collection of Japanese art and archeology, plus Chinese, Korean, and Central Asian art treasures *(see pp24–7)*.

Yanaka 9
Ueno Park 6 5
Matsugaya 2
Asakusa
KOTOTOI-DORI
KOTOTOI-DORI
Ueno
ASAKUSA-DORI
EDO-DORI
BUNKYO-KU
TAITO-KU
SUMIDA-KU
Taito
KURAMAEBASHI-DORI
KOKUSAI-DORI
EXPRESSWAY NO.6
7
YUSHIMA ZAKA
Yanagibashi
Yokoami
Ichigaya
Fujimi
Jinbocho
Kanda
Yokoami
Kajicho
Ryogoku
KEIYO-DORI
Tatekawa
EXPRESSWAY NO.5
YASUKUNI-DORI
CHUO-DORI
EDO-DORI
Hamacho 3
Rokubancho
Imperial Palace East Gardens
Otemachi
CHUO-KU
Tokiwa
Sumida River
SHINJUKU-DORI
CHIYODA-KU 1
Nihonbashi
EITAI-DORI
Kioicho
HIBIYA-DORI
CHUO-DORI
SHOWA-DORI
Nagatacho
Marunouchi
Shinkawa
Hibiya Park
Ginza
10 5 miles
Akasaka

Koishikawa Korakuen Garden 7
Tokyo's oldest garden has many features, including a heart-shaped pond and quaint bridges – all rife with symbolism *(see pp28–9)*.

Meiji Shrine 8
Sited in a forest, the exquisite Shinto architecture of shrine buildings and an iris garden embody the theme of nature *(see pp30–31)*.

Yanaka 9
Set around a leafy cemetery, this neighborhood retains the atmosphere of historic Tokyo, with its temples, shrines, and traditional shopping streets. *(see pp32–3)*.

Odaiba Island 10
With high-tech buildings, exhibition sites, museums, fashion malls, a Ferris wheel, and a man-made beach, the artificial island of Odaiba is a place of entertainment and experiment *(see pp34–5)*.

🔟 ⭐ Imperial Palace Grounds

Located at the center of one of the largest cities in the developed world, the Imperial Palace grounds sit amid a galaxy of busy urban areas. This enormous compound contains the magnificent residence of the emperor, along with a variety of moats, stone walls, watchtowers, gates, and fairytale bridges. The public areas of the grounds are also home to several museums, galleries, and beautiful Japanese gardens. This is a solemn spot, resonating with cultural meaning, and is among the few places where one can witness the incredible persistence of history.

1 Sakurada-mon Gate

This entrance to the outer gardens was erected in 1457. A survivor of earthquakes, fires, and air raids, the entrance consists of two structures: one, a broad inner gate, is angled at 90-degrees to thwart intruders.

2 National Museum of Modern Art, Tokyo

More than 12,000 works by Japanese as well as Western artists are exhibited here, dating from the 19th century to the present day. Works include the beautiful *Mother and Child* by Uemura Shoen (above).

3 Ote-mon Gate and Nijubashi Bridge

South of Ote-mon gate, the 1888 reconstructed Nijubashi Bridge (above) is a graceful sight. The bridge is a popular backdrop for photos.

4 Imperial Palace East Gardens

Designed by Kobori Enshu in the early 17th century, these gardens (right) feature stone lanterns, bridges, ponds, swathes of flowers, and towering zelkova trees.

5 Shiomizaka

Stone walls line the path up to the "Tide View Slope." The small promontory once commanded fine views of the sea and Mount Fuji.

6 Imperial Palace Plaza

The plaza's pristine lawns, cherry trees, and stands of ornamental black pines were laid out in 1899. The gravel concourse acts as a firebreak. The plaza offers lovely views of Nijubashi Bridge.

Imperial Palace Grounds

TRAUMAS IN THE GARDENS

The tranquil gardens of today's palace grounds have known their fair share of drama. Victims of the great 1923 earthquake sheltered here. During the war, several members of Japan's officer corps, inconsolable at news of their nation's defeat, came here in August 1945 to commit ritual suicide. In the 1950s and 1960s, the plaza witnessed violent political demonstrations.

8 Nippon Budokan

The colossal octagonal roof of the Budokan, or Japan Martial Arts Hall, features onion-shaped finials covered in gold leaf. Its elements mirror those seen in traditional Japanese temples.

10 Crafts Gallery

The former headquarters of the Imperial Guard, this 1910 government-listed structure is now a gallery showcasing the work of Japanese craftspeople.

7 Wadakura Fountain Park

The sprays and jets of this striking aquatic park, built in 1961 to commemorate the wedding of the present emperor's parents, were refurbished in 1995.

9 Chidorigafuchi

The stone walls of the shogun's former castle contrast with the inky waters of Chidorigafuchi moat **(above)**, which is home to turtles, carp, cormorants, egrets, and gliding swans.

NEED TO KNOW

MAP K1–M4 ▪ Chiyoda, Chiyoda-ku ▪ www.kunaicho. go.jp/eindex.html

Adm for museums and galleries

▪ All museums in the complex are closed on Mondays (except for public holidays). Try to visit the grounds early: the tour groups turn up by mid-morning. The best plum and cherry blossom viewing is from February to mid-April, and azaleas and dogwood in mid-May.

▪ Picnics are permitted in Kitanomaru Park, but it's better to cross the road south of the palace grounds for Hibiya Park, where an outdoor café serves sandwiches, noodles, and even decent British fish and chips.

TOP 10 ★ Senso-ji Temple

Rebuilt countless times since its founding in 628, Senso-ji is the oldest temple site in Tokyo and the capital's spiritual epicenter. The current temple, dedicated to Kannon, the Goddess of Mercy, is a fireproof replica of an earlier version built in 1692. One of the liveliest spots in the city, its grounds attract throngs of visitors, who come to pray inside its cavernous main hall with its opulent, golden altar and priceless collection of 18th- and 19th-century votive paintings. This religious sanctuary lies at the heart of a busy commercial and entertainment district.

1 Kaminari-mon Gate
The "Thunder Gate" is flanked by two gods: Fujin and Raijin. A red paper lantern with the character for "thunder" emblazoned on it hangs within **(above)**.

3 Niten-mon Gate
The 1618 ox-blood-colored gate on the east side is a designated an Important Cultural Treasure. Its pillars and walls are covered with votive papers stuck there by the faithful.

4 Giant Straw Sandals
Two large straw sandals hang on the Hozomon Treasury Gate. Made for deities with feet of mythic size, they symbolize the traditional footwear of the Buddhist pilgrim.

5 Nakamise-dori
The main avenue to the city's holiest sanctuary is packed with more than 150 stalls and booths selling traditional goods and souvenirs.

2 Incense Burner
A giant bronze incense burner **(above)** stands in front of the main hall. The faithful burn pink sticks of incense, wafting the smoke over their clothes for good luck.

NEED TO KNOW

MAP R2 ■ 2-3-1 Asakusa, Taito-ku ■ 3842-0181
■ www.senso-ji.jp

Open 24 hrs daily

■ The temple grounds get crowded, so make an early start on the sights.

■ Combine a trip to the temple with a Sumida River cruise from Azuma Bridge.

■ Grab an outside table at one of the many local backstreet restaurants to the west of the temple for an early lunch.

6 Senso-ji Main Hall

Senso-ji Temple's main hall **(below)** has a lavish interior, the centerpiece of which is a richly decorated gold and lacquer altar. Walls have votive paintings and the ceiling has a colorful dragon motif surrounded by angels and lotuses.

Senso-ji Temple

DENBOIN-DORI

NAKAMISE-DORI

UMAMICHI-DORI

Asakusa

KAMINARIMON-DORI

MYSTERY OF THE GOLDEN KANNON

On March 18, 628, two fishermen brothers found a golden statue of the goddess Kannon in their nets. The 2-inch (5-cm) image is today enshrined in Senso-ji. At the moment of discovery, according to legend, a golden dragon danced from heaven to earth. A Golden Dragon Dance is held in the temple grounds every spring and fall to mark the occasion.

9 Nade Jizo

This bronze bodhisattva statue **(above)**, a figure of compassion, is believed to relieve ailments if you rub the part of its body that troubles you.

7 Denbo-in Garden

This tranquil garden **(below)** was designed in the early 1600s by the Zen gardener Kobori Enshu. Tea ceremonies are performed in a small pavilion beside the pond.

8 Benten Mound

Dedicated to Benten, goddess of beauty and the arts, a red shrine sits atop a hill built over an ancient burial mound. A bell rings for the opening of the temple grounds.

10 Asakusa Jinja

At the entrance to the 1649 shrine's main hall sit protective lion-dog statues **(above)**, which honor two men who found an image of the goddess Kannon in their fishing nets.

⭐ Sumida River

The Sumida River, Tokyo's premier waterway, has long been a symbol of the city. While its water and embankments are a setting for commerce, festivals, gardens, bridges, and ferries, its literary associations form a rich body of lore. The girders, shackles, and bolts of older bridges, with their sweeping arches, stone stanchions, and wrought-iron lanterns, lend a sense of continuity to the ever-changing Tokyo. Low-hulled sculls operated by oarsmen have now given way to waterbuses and pleasure boats.

1 Kiyosu Bridge
Built in 1928, this blue bridge **(above)** was inspired by one that once crossed the Rhine in Cologne. Its eight lanterns are lit at twilight.

2 Asahi Beer Hall
Set above Azuma Bridge, this striking black building **(above)**, designed by Philippe Starck, is in the form of an inverted pyramid. Even more surreal is the rooftop installation known as the *Flamme d'Or*.

3 Tsukuda-jima
The first residents of this island congregated at Sumiyoshi Shrine, which is dedicated to Sumiyoshi Myojin, protector of seafarers.

4 Yanagi Bridge
This green bridge, standing proudly at the heart of an old geisha district, has bolted plates in the southern Chuo Ward and north-facing panels in Taito Ward. House boats and fishing boats are moored here.

5 Komagata Bridge
The curving blue girders and stone stanchions of this 1927 bridge combine strength and elegance. The span's eight lanterns are lit at twilight, creating one of the city's most romantic nighttime scenes.

6 Eitai Bridge
Convicts were once loaded onto boats from this bridge **(above)** and shipped off to Japan's penal colonies. It offers sweeping scenic river views.

RIVER FIREWORKS

Since 1732, the Sumida River around Asakusa has hosted spectacular firework displays. On the last Saturday of July, tens of thousands of pyrotechnic wonders illuminate the night sky between the Sakura and Umaya bridges as firework manufacturers strive to outdo one another. Arrive very early to secure prime view spots (or book a cruise on a boat), as the festival attracts around one million spectators.

9 Umaya Bridge
This imposing steel structure is named after the shogun's horse stables, once located west of the bridge. Bas-relief horses appear on the ornamental pillars.

7 Basho Inari Shrine and Statue
Dedicated to the haiku poet Matsuo Basho (1644–94), this shrine leads to an elevated garden with a seated statue of him.

8 Hama Rikyu Garden
Features of the original garden can be seen in the tidal pond, in islets linked by wooden bridges, and in a tea pavilion. The pond is home to saltwater fish.

NEED TO KNOW

Asakusa Pier: **MAP R2**
Hama Rikyu Pier: **MAP N6**

■ The best way to see the river highlights is to take a water bus *(see p120)* between Asakusa and Hama Rikyu Garden, or a little farther on to Odaiba Island. Enthusiasts of the poet Basho can stroll just north of the Basho Inari Shrine to the Basho Memorial Museum, a research center with manuscripts, calligraphy, and illustrations of scenes from his life.

■ Next to Ryogoku JR station, Popeye is an excellent place to stop for German- and Japanese-style snacks and craft beer.

10 Tokyo Skytree
The world's tallest free-standing tower has observation decks at two levels, along with a restaurant. It dazzles most when illuminated at night **(above)**.

TOP 10 ⭐ Edo-Tokyo Museum

Charting the history of Edo and Tokyo, the Edo-Tokyo Museum is housed in an elevated building that resembles an intergalactic space station on stilts. Its height, which dwarfs every other building nearby, matches that of former Edo Castle, and the raised edifice is modeled after a traditional Japanese rice storehouse. More modern touches include the red escalator that rises from the terrace to the underbelly of the cantilevered upper stories, and the panels coated with fluorine resin. Highlights include a replica of Nihonbashi bridge and an evocative reconstruction of the 1945 air raids that ravaged Tokyo.

Ginza Streetscape ①

This museum exhibits a number of small-scale models, such as this one **(right)** of the Ginza district during the Meiji era (1868– 1912). This shows Ginza when Western-style architecture had started to make a big impact on Tokyo.

② Photos of Edo-Meiji Periods

Sepia-toned images of samurais and rickshaw pullers became outdated during the Meiji era. These gave way to photos of Western-style hotels, streetcars, exhibition sites, and factories along the Sumida River.

③ Life of Artisans and Townspeople

The life of ordinary people can be seen in the models of townspeople's residences and the well-crafted mock-ups of the commercial city on the fifth floor.

④ Districts

Models on the sixth floor show the Edo-era residential districts. The fifth floor features villages and river islands connected to Edo.

⑤ Daimyo Lodgings

The sixth-floor model of the grand estates of *daimyo* (feudal lords) was skillfully reconstructed from old prints and plans.

⑥ Nihonbashi Bridge

The sixth floor leads directly onto a reconstructed section of Nihonbashi bridge. The carpentry and joinery of the original bridge, which was rebuilt several times, can be seen in the replica.

⑦ Portable Festival Floats

Exquisite *mikoshi* **(left)** are crafted for use at traditional festivals. The portable floats are gold-plated and encrusted with precious stones.

9 Row House Tenement

Today's living conditions in Tokyo may be a little cramped, but during the Edo period townspeople had to make do with inconceivably small homes **(left)**. An example of a typical tenement row house from this era can be viewed on the fifth floor of the museum.

NEED TO KNOW

MAP H3 ◾ 1-4-1 Yokoami, Sumida-ku ◾ 3626-9974 ◾ Ryogoku, Toei Oedo subway, JR Sobu Line ◾ www.edo-tokyo-museum.or.jp

Open 9:30am–5:30pm Tue–Sun (to 7:30pm Sat) and public holidays

Adm

◾ A small, refundable deposit is required for borrowing earphones that provide audio commentary.

◾ Volunteer guides are available for tours in English, French, German, Spanish, Chinese, and Korean. Call the museum at least 2 weeks in advance to reserve a guide.

◾ The Japanese restaurant-café Sakura-Saryo on the seventh floor serves modern takes on Edo-period recipes

Museum Guide

Ticket counters are on the first floor beneath the main building, and outside on the third-floor terrace to the left of the main building.

An escalator takes visitors up to the permanent exhibitions on the fifth and sixth floors. The sixth floor focuses on the Edo-period city, and the fifth floor explores Edo's later years and transition to Tokyo.

Descend to the first floor for special exhibitions and the impressive museum store.

There is also a Sumida Ward souvenir store featuring local crafts.

8 Kabuki Theater

On the fifth floor, this superb replica of the Nakamura-za Kabuki theater recreates stage scenes from the mid-17th century, animated by life-size models **(above)** of all-male actors.

10 Woodblock Printing

Re-creations of a printing shop and Edo-era book-store on the fifth floor are complemented by display cases containing printing equipment, books, and woodblock prints.

TOP10 ⭐ Ueno Park

Home to one of the most impressive concentrations of high art in the city, Ueno Park sits at the center of a down-to-earth working-class residential and entertainment district. With its temples, shrines, cherry trees, a magnificent lotus pond, statues, and tombs, the park is like a miniature model of Japan. The hill, on which the upper part of the park sits, was once a great religious center. During the Meiji and Taisho periods, this historical stage served as a venue for large-scale art and industrial exhibitions, paving the way for the venerable museums and galleries that occupy the park today. Huge numbers gather here during the spring cherry-blossom season.

1 **Ueno Zoo**
Built in 1882, this zoo is home to giant pandas, Indian lions, Sumatran tigers, and other critters. A monorail ride leads to a tamer petting section.

2 **Toshogu Shrine and Kara-mon Gate**
This opulent shrine **(right)**, dedicated to the first shogun, Tokugawa Ieyasu, was renovated in 1651. A row of stone and copper lanterns leads to the shrine.

NEED TO KNOW

MAP F1–F2 ■ Ueno Park, Taito-ku

Open 24 hrs daily

■ Those interested in art can combine a visit to the park with a trip to the Taikan Yokoyama Memorial Hall, the painter's private house, which stands opposite Shinobazu Pond.

■ The causeway leading from the large *torii* (gate) to Benten island is lined with stalls. This is a great place to sample traditional snacks and light dishes.

3 **National Museum of Western Art**
Designed by Le Corbusier, the museum's exhibits range from 15th-century religious pieces to works by Pollock and Miro.

4 **Gojo Tenjin and Hanazono Inari Fox Shrines**
Winding paths lead through red *torii* (gates) **(right)** to Gojo and Hanazono shrines. Inari fox statues stand inside.

5 Cherry Trees
Every spring, the park hosts Tokyo's largest cherry-blossom party **(above)**. Beer, sake, dancing, and karaoke are the main highlights.

MEIJI RESTORATION

A fierce battle between supporters of the deposed shogun and the new forces of the Meiji restoration was fought on Ueno Hill in 1868. Heavy rains flooded Shinobazu Pond, with men combating in knee-deep water, while a cannon shot from a teahouse on one side of the water and another from a cave dedicated to Inari exploded over their heads. Over 300 men died in the conflict.

9 Benten-do
This temple honors the Goddess of Beauty **(left)**. The ceiling inside the hall is painted with dragons, and the walls with murals of fall flowers.

10 Shinobazu Pond
The pond's southern section is filled with pink lotuses during the summer. Reeds provide a habitat for herons, grebes, and thousands of other water fowl.

6 Saigo Takamori Statue
The bronze statue, unveiled in 1898, is a tribute to Takamori, a powerful samurai who led a major rebellion in the 19th century. He is shown wearing a summer kimono, walking his dog.

7 Five-Story Pagoda
Covered with bronze roof tiles to protect it from fire, the current pagoda was built in 1640. The 120-ft- (37-m-) tall vermillion structure is located inside the zoo.

8 Shitamachi Museum
Displaying a range of everyday items such as kitchenware, tools, and furniture, this museum also features re-creations of Edo-era stores and tenements.

Tokyo National Museum

Occupying a major part of the northern reaches of Ueno Park, the colossal Tokyo National Museum was known in the prewar period as the Imperial Household Museum. This magisterial museum, set among courtyards, fountains, and trees, is divided into four main galleries: Honkan, Heiseikan, Toyokan, and Gallery of Horyu-ji Treasures. These contain not only the most important collection of Japanese art and archeology in the world, but a treasure trove of Asian antiquities as well. The main galleries display almost 3,000 items at any one time – a huge amount to see in one visit. There is a garden on the side of the Honkan which opens for the cherry blossom and fall foliage seasons.

Japanese Paintings and Prints **1**

The Honkan features paintings from the classical Heian to Muromachi periods, as well as fine examples of mural, screen, and paper door art, and Zen-inspired ink landscapes. The highlight of the Edo era is the work of its *ukiyo-e* woodblock print artists **(right)**.

Ceramics **2**
Japanese ceramics **(above)** in the Honkan are represented by Kyoto and Imari ware. The Toyokan has Chinese ceramics from the Song to Qing dynasties.

Lacquerware **3**
Included among the Japanese National Treasures and Important Cultural Properties exhibited in the Honkan are stunning *maki-e* lacquerware items dating from the Heian to Edo periods.

The Gallery of Horyu-ji Treasures **4**
This invaluable art collection of more than 300 objects, including a forest of standing bodhisattvas from Horyu-ji temple, Nara, is exhibited here.

Previous pages Detail of an artifact displayed at the Edo-Tokyo Museum

8 Textiles

The Toyokan has a sumptuous collection of textiles from China, Korea, Southeast Asia, Central Asia, India, and Egypt. The exquisite Indonesian brocade work made from gold thread can also be seen here **(left)**. The Honkan houses Japanese textiles.

5 Japanese Archeology

The Heiseikan, dedicated to Japanese archeology, houses relics from the Jomon period (c.10,000–300 BC) onward. The chronology of Japanese arts can be found here.

6 Asian Arts

The Toyokan is the gallery to see Asian art. The collection includes fine examples of Korean metalwork, Khmer pottery, Hindu statuary, and cave paintings from the grottoes of Bingling, China.

9 Arms and Armor

The equipment once owned by Japan's military elite is displayed in the Honkan. Often excessively embellished, this includes the warriors' attire: armor, helmets, saddlery, and sword mountings.

7 Calligraphy

The master calligraphy in the Honkan includes *bokuseki*, executed by Zen priests **(above)**. Even if the meanings of the Chinese characters elude you, the beauty of the brushwork will not.

NEED TO KNOW

MAP F1 ■ 13-9 Ueno Park, Taito-ku ■ 3822-1111 ■ www.tnm.jp

Open 9:30am–5pm Tue–Sun (until 9pm Fri & Sat); Apr–Sep: until 6pm Sun & public holidays

Adm

■ The museum shop on the first floor of the Honkan sells items linked to museum exhibits and motifs.

■ The Hotel Okura Garden terrace in The Gallery of Horyu-ji is a pleasant setting for lunch. There are cheaper options at the stalls and cafés in Ueno Park.

Museum Guide
The main gate to the museum complex, consisting of four major galleries, lies at the north end of Ueno Park. The central gallery, the Honkan, is straight ahead, beyond the pond. The Toyokan is on the right, and the Heiseikan is to the left, behind the Honkan. The Gallery of Horyu-ji Treasures lies to the left of the main gate, behind the Hyokeikan, a grand building open only for special exhibits and events.

10 Religious Sculptures

Religious sculptures **(left)** are scattered throughout the galleries. Bronze, gilt, and sandstone sculptures from Pakistan are exhibited in the Toyokan. The Honkan displays Buddhist statues from India and Japan.

Galleries and Outdoor Features

Exterior of the Honkan, which contains Japanese art and artifacts

1 Honkan

The main gallery and center-piece of Ueno Park was designed by Jin Watanabe. The present Honkan was completed in 1938 in the "Imperial Crown" style of architecture. The features are Japanese, but the building materials are undeniably Western.

2 Toyokan

Asian artworks and archeological exhibits are housed in a light, modernist building. Parts of the collection may sometimes be shown elsewhere within the complex.

Teahouse in the museum garden

3 Museum Garden and Teahouses

The site is open to the public during the spring cherry-blossom or fall leaf-viewing seasons. Those who are in Tokyo around this time should not pass up the chance to see the secret pond-garden and teahouses on the north side of the Honkan.

4 Heiseikan

Opened in 1999 – with a sleek courtyard, auditorium, and lounge – this modern gallery houses pottery, burial statues, and artifacts from the ancient world.

5 Shiryokan

The Shiryokan is a research and information center, where visitors can browse through archives, books, magazines, monochrome and color photographs, and other materials linked to art history.

6 Gallery of Horyu-ji Treasures

The minimalist 1999 design of this gallery is the work of Yoshio Taniguchi, whose overseas projects include the groundbreaking Museum of Modern Art (MOMA) in New York.

7 Black Gate

A rare structure from the Edo period, the Kuro-mon is topped with a heavy hip-and-gable style roof. Old roof tiles and foundation stones are kept in the rear of the gate.

8 Azekura Sutra Store

Buddhist sutras were once kept in stores like this one, transported in 1882 from Gango-ji temple in Nara. Constructed of logs, the inner walls

ASIAN ART THEMES

With over 110,000 objects in its collection, the Tokyo National Museum regularly rotates its exhibits. The Tokyokan consists of 10 exhibition rooms divided by regional themes. The themes listed opposite at the Toyokan are part of its permanent collection, but individual displays change.

This Gandharan sculpture is one of the highlights of the collection housed in the Toyokan.

STONE AGE TOKYO

Early settlers lived along the ridges and bluffs of the present-day Yamanote Hills. From here, they had ready access to plentiful supplies of fish and shellfish. A pre-Bronze Age site – the Omori shell mound – in southwest Tokyo was discovered in 1877 by the American zoologist Edward Sylvester Morse. The event marked the beginning of Japanese archeology.

TOP 10 ASIAN ART THEMES

1 Indian and Gandharan Sculpture (13th–2nd century BC)

2 Ancient Asian Bronze Drums (6th–5th century BC)

3 West Asian Textiles (19th century)

4 Chinese Archeology (2nd–1st century BC)

5 Chinese Textiles (15th–17th century)

6 Chinese Ceramics (Three Kingdoms period–Tang dynasty)

7 Chinese Ceramics (Song–Qing dynasty)

8 Chinese Stone Reliefs from Shangdong (1st–2nd century)

9 Korean Ceramics (9th–10th century)

10 Central Asian Religious Cave Paintings (Tang dynasty)

of this tiny storehouse are decorated with murals depicting bodhisattvas and protective deities.

9 Hyokeikan

A prized example of a Meiji-era Western-style building, the white stone walls and green domes of this Important Cultural Property are an impressive if somewhat sober sight.

10 Statue of Edward Jenner

British physician Edward Jenner (1749–1823) was the pioneer of vaccination. This memorial statue by Yonehara Unkai, a pupil of sculptor Koun Takamura, was erected in 1896 as a tribute to Jenner and his great achievement.

The Hyokeikan, built in 1909

TOP 10 ⭐ Koishikawa Korakuen Garden

Established in 1629, Tokyo's oldest surviving garden was commissioned by Tokugawa Yorifusa, lord of the Mito branch of the Tokugawa family. Its designer, Tokudaiji Sahei, was aided by the Confucian scholar, Zhu Shunshui, a Chinese refugee from the fall of the Ming dynasty. The garden was once a recreational space for the Tokugawa clan to entertain guests, clamber up its miniature hills, float in barges on its pond, and stage poetry parties.

1 Mount Lu and Lotuses

Miniature landscapes here recall famous places in poetry and mythology. Below this imitation of Mount Lu in China **(above)** is a sacred lotus pond.

NEED TO KNOW

MAP E2 ■ 1-6-6 Koraku, Bunkyo-ku ■ 3811-3015 ■ www.tokyo-park.or.jp/english/park

Open 9am–5pm

Adm

■ Try to get to the garden when it opens, before the amusement park next door gets into full swing. In the fierce summer months the garden is much cooler at this time as well.

■ Kantoku-tei, a teahouse with a room facing onto Oigawa river, serves *matcha* (powdered green tea) along with a traditional Japanese confection.

2 Horai-jima Island

The island at the pond's center represents the Taoist paradise of Horai-jima. The idea of a "heavenly isle" in a garden was conceived by the Chinese Emperor Wu.

3 Engetsukyo Bridge

A stroll along the winding, tree-sheltered paths leads to the Chinese-style Engetsukyo **(below)**, the "round moon bridge," arguably the oldest ornamental stone bridge in Tokyo.

4 Tsuiji Walls

The current wall is a reinforced concrete imitation of the original *tsuiji* plastered walls, but moss and staining from Tokyo's steamy summers have given the newer walls a patina of age.

5 Symbolic Rice Field

Created to show the hardships faced by peasant farmers, a rice field lies to the north of the garden. School kids plant and harvest the crop.

6 Kuhachiya House

Standing in the middle of a glade of red pines, this thatched-roof building is modeled on an Edo-era drinking house.

9 Inner Garden
Apart from a long-gone Chinese gate, everything else remains the same as when the Mito family used this Chinese-style inner garden as a sanctum and place of study.

7 Tsutenkyo Bridge
Spanning a deep ravine and supported on piles, the bridge **(above)** is a replica of a structure in Tofuku-ji, a temple complex in Kyoto. Its reflection in the shallow river amplifies its size.

8 Iris Garden
Planted in the marsh surrounding the zigzag bridge, purple and white Japanese and rabbit-ear irises bloom during the June rainy season. An ancient system of sluice gates and dikes irrigates the marsh.

10 Plum Orchard and Yatsu-hashi
An attractive plum orchard **(above)** just to the north of the pond comes into fragrant white blossom in early February. Nearby, a zigzag, eight-span *yatsu-hashi* bridge runs through a small marsh.

Koishikawa Korakuen Garden

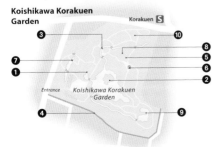

Korakuen **S**

❸ ❿

❼ ❽
❺
❶ ❻
❷

Entrance Koishikawa Korakuen Garden

❹ ❾

TOP 10 ⭐ Meiji Shrine

Dedicated to the memory of Emperor Meiji (1852–1912) and his wife, Empress Shoken, Meiji Shrine is a fine example of restrained Shinto architecture. Completed in 1921, the shrine was destroyed in an air raid in 1945. The current reconstruction is indistinguishable from the original. The gravel paths and courtyards of the grounds host cultural events, ranging from Noh and Kyogen drama, court dances, and music performances to horseback archery, winter ice sculptures, and calligraphy shows.

3 Main Shrine
This elegant and classic Shinto-style shrine **(right)** can be entered through one of three decorated, wooden gates.

4 Imperial Treasure House
This collection of personal artifacts belongs to the Meiji royalty. A painting by the Italian artist Ugolini depicts the emperor in European military dress, with a vase standing on a table at his side. The same vase stands next to the painting in the museum.

1 Torii
The 39-ft (12-m) main gate **(above)** is Japan's largest torii. It was constructed from 1,500-year-old Japanese *hinoki* cypress trees transported from Alishan mountain in Taiwan.

2 Ichi no Torii
Meaning "first gate," this torii is positioned at the main entrance to Meiji Shrine. Torii symbolize the perch where a mythological cock sat before it announced the dawn that lured the sun goddess Amaterasu from her cave. The 16-petal chrysanthemum medallions at the top of the gate are a symbol of the imperial family.

NEED TO KNOW
MAP B5 ▪ 1-1 Kamizonocho, Yoyogi, Shibuya-ku ▪ 3379-5511 ▪ Harajuku, Harajuku JR Yamanote Line; Meiji-Jingumae, Chiyoda Line ▪ www.meijijingu.or.jp/english

Main Shrine: Dawn to dusk

Iris Garden: 9am–4pm (to 4:30pm Mar–Oct); adm

Imperial Treasure House: Sat–Sun, public holidays and festival days; adm

▪ Comfortable shoes are recommended for the shrine, with a 10-minute walk along a gravel path.

▪ The boundary of adjacent Yoyogi Park (*see p49*) has stalls selling snacks, light meals, and other refreshments.

EMPEROR MEIJI
In 1867, two British emissaries, Sir Harry Parkes and Algernon Mitford, were granted an audience with the 15-year-old emperor in his palace in Kyoto. What they found was a vision of medieval sovereignty: a boy dressed in white brocade and silk trousers, his teeth lacquered black, eyebrows shaved, and cheeks painted red. Less than a year later, he would proclaim the Meiji era and by the end of his reign, Japan was an industrialized nation, strong enough to have defeated Russia in 1904–5.

5 Votive Tablets

Hung on prayer boards in front of the shrine **(right)**, *ema* (votive tablets sending prayers to the god) are still popular, especially among students petitioning for divine help in passing exams. Another *ema* is usually hung in gratitude, if a wish is fulfilled.

8 JR Bridge

The bridge leading to the shrine is a free zone for performance artists, some of whom enjoy dressing up in rococo hairstyles and gothic makeup.

10 Meiji Shrine Iris Garden

A wooded path leads into a sunken garden **(below)**, bordered by misty woods and thatched gazebos. In early June, purple, pink, and white irises bloom in the water garden.

6 Traditional Wedding Processions

Along with the many other rituals and dedicatory ceremonies held at the shrine, Shinto weddings **(above)** are quietly formal in manner and attire, but visually dazzling. Most weddings take place on Saturday afternoons.

7 Evergreen Forest

Much of the grounds are densely forested. More than 120,000 trees and shrubs form a natural garden of Japanese flora.

9 Souvenir Store

Amulets, incense, talismans, lucky arrows, key rings strung with a tiny shrine bell, and models of tanuki (raccoon-dog deity) are sold here.

TOP10 ⭐ Yanaka

An oasis of calm, seemingly frozen in time, Yanaka is a far cry from the idea of Tokyo as a metropolis of the future. The area, a short stroll north of Ueno Park but easily accessed from Nippori Station on the JR Yamanote line, is where some 60 temples and shrines relocated after a fire devastated the city's downtown area in 1657. They remain there today alongside the elegiac Yanaka Cemetery, the last resting place of many of the city's luminaries, and Yanaka Ginza, a traditional shopping street straight out of Tokyo's past.

1 **Yanaka Ginza**
Global chains are banished from this shopping street in favor of stores selling meat and groceries, cafés **(above)**, *soba* restaurants, and crafts stores such as Yanaka Matsunoya, which sells artisan-made household goods.

2 **Suwa Shrine**
At New Year, the grounds of this 1202 shrine on the edge of a plateau are strung with lanterns showing the animal zodiac sign for the coming year.

3 **Zensho-an Temple**
Every August, this Zen meditation temple displays its collection of painted scrolls depicting supernatural folk tales.

4 **Daien-ji Temple**
This temple has a Buddhist and a Shinto hall. Its Chrysanthemum Festival is held here annually on October 14–15, when dolls made from flowers are displayed and puppet performances take place.

6 **Tenno-ji Temple**
Founded in 1274, this temple contains the Great Buddha of Yanaka **(above)**, a fine bronze statue cast in 1690.

5 **Yanaka Cemetery**
The graves of the last shogun **(above)**, Tokugawa Yoshinobu (1837-1913), and the infamous murderess Takahashi Oden are among the many famous figures buried in this cemetery.

8 Isetatsu

This 1864 shop **(left)** creates *chiyogami* – patterned *washi* (Japanese handmade paper) once popular with the samurai class. Today, the paper is used for decorative purposes and origami.

GREAT BUDDHA OF YANAKA

Tokyoites have a special affection for their very own Great Buddha of Yanaka. The 16-ft (5-m) statue belongs to Tenno-ji temple, a sanctuary that was damaged during the Battle of Ueno (1868) *(see p21)*. The fact that the statue survived added to its mystic appeal. Cast in bronze in 1690, this Chinese-style figure has finely carved facial features, representing the Shaka-nyorai Buddha. It stands in a tranquil corner of the temple precincts, among lush surroundings.

10 Asakura Museum of Sculpture

The former home and studio of sculptor Fumio Asakura (1883–1964) contains many of his graceful statues.

7 Ueno Sakuragi Atari

Get a glimpse of life in the Edo period: three traditional wooden houses built in 1938 have been converted into a beer hall, a bakery, two stores, and a community space.

9 Daimyo Clock Museum

This interesting museum displays timepieces made for the privileged classes during the Edo era. The 12 signs of the Chinese zodiac were used to indicate the hour.

NEED TO KNOW

MAP F1

Ueno Sakuragi Atari: opening times vary, check website for details; www.uenosakuragiatari.jp

Isetatsu: open 10am–6pm; www.isetatsu.com

Daimyo Clock Museum: 3821-6913; open 10am– 4pm Mon–Sat; closed Jul–Sep; adm

Asakura Museum of Sculpture: 3821-4549; open 9:30am–4:30pm Tue–Wed, Fri–Sun; adm

■ Yanaka is full of free art galleries. Drop by SCAI – The Bathhouse *(see p47)*, which is located in a

former bathhouse; Oguraya (7-6-8 Yanaka), set in a building dating from 1847; and Edokoro (1-6-17 Yanaka; www. allanwest.jp), the studio of artist Allan West, who is well-known for making gilded screens and scrolls inspired by nature.

TOP 10 ⭐ Odaiba Island

When coastal megacities run out of space, they inevitably turn toward the sea. An aerial view of Tokyo reveals a city stretched to its limits, coming to a congested stop at the waterfront. Geometrically precise islands appear, seemingly lowered into place like space panels. As well as exhibition pavilions, indoor shopping malls, game centers, cafés, restaurants, and surrealistic constructions of Odaiba Island, visitors are intrigued by the structures on this landfill that seem to hail from the future rather than the past.

1 Rainbow Bridge
At night, this graceful bridge **(above)** is illuminated and in summer fireworks displays are held on the waters around the bridge's stanchions.

DEFENDING THE BAY
The Edo-era Tokugawa government built man-made islands as cannon batteries to protect Tokyo from foreign invasion. The fear was well founded. In the 1850s, heavily armed American steamships, led by Commodore Perry, moored close offshore (see p38). In all, five islands were built. Today, only Battery Island Nos. 3 and 6 remain.

2 Palette Town
This complex includes the Venus Fort shopping mall, a Ferris wheel illuminated at night with rainbow colors, and the Toyota car showroom Mega Web, where you can enjoy simulated rides.

3 RiSuPia
Electronics giant Panasonic shows off its latest gadgets and has a great hands-on science and discovery center, which is a fun distraction for kids and adults.

4 Oedo Onsen Monogatari
Dip into tepid to scalding natural spring waters, indoor and outdoor tubs, a steaming sand bath, sauna, foot massage pool, or bed of hot stones at this rejuvenating hot-spring complex **(below)**.

Odaiba Island

9 National Museum of Emerging Science and Innovation

Laid out in a futuristic building, this museum focuses on space, life sciences, and cutting-edge technology **(below)**.

6 DiverCity Tokyo Plaza

Lovers of Japanese pop culture will delight at the statue of the anime robot Gundam in front of this mega-shopping mall, which has a Gundam-themed exhibition hall.

7 Tokyo Big Sight

The megalithic exhibition center has an eighth-floor observation space. The gravity-defying structure consists of four inverted pyramids standing on a seemingly narrow base.

10 Decks and Aqua City

Decks is a boulevard of outdoor patios and restaurants. Next door, Aqua City has a trick art museum, Legoland, and Madame Tussauds.

5 Odaiba Marine Park

A man-made beach and a replica of New York's Statue of Liberty are among the attractions of this park, along with mesmerizing views of the city skyline and Rainbow Bridge.

8 Fuji TV Building

Two blocks of this Kenzo Tange-designed building **(above)** are joined by girder-like sky corridors and a titanium-paneled sphere. The Observation Deck offers the finest view of Tokyo.

NEED TO KNOW

MAP D2

Palette Town: 3529-1821; www.palette-town.com

RiSuPia: 3599-2600; open 10am–6pm Tue–Sun; adm

Oedo Onsen Monogatari: 5500-1126; open 11am–9pm; adm

National Museum of Emerging Science and Innovation: 3570-9151; open 10am–5pm, Wed–Mon; adm

Tokyo Big Sight: 5530-1111

Fuji TV Building: 5500-8888; open 10am–6pm daily; adm

DiverCity Tokyo Plaza: 6380-7800; open 10am–11pm; www.divercity-tokyo.com/en

■ The island gets packed on weekends. Weekdays are usually quieter.

■ Grab a bite at the food theme park of Odaiba Takoyaki Museum in Decks.

The Top 10 of Everything

Shinjuku Gyoen Garden in fall

🔟 Moments in History

Senso-ji in 1904, before the air raids

1 Founding of Senso-ji Temple

Discovered by two fishermen in their nets in 628, the golden image of the goddess Kannon was enshrined at the site of present-day Senso-ji. The temple has been rebuilt several times, and after air raids in 1945 a replica was put up in ferroconcrete.

2 Ota Dokan's Fort

The Musashino Plain was developed into a martial domain with the arrival of Ota Dokan, a minor feudal lord, in 1456. Dokan's fortress was built on a site named Edo, meaning "estuary mouth." A statue of the city founder stands at the Tokyo International Forum in Yurakucho.

3 Founding of Edo

The development of Edo village into Japan's de facto military capital began when future shogun Tokugawa Ieyasu arrived there in 1590. The land was reclaimed, water courses expanded, residences built, and a huge citadel, Edo Castle, was erected.

4 Long-Sleeves Fire

In 1657, priests at Hommyo-ji temple in Hongo burned a "cursed" kimono owned by three girls who had died before becoming old enough to wear it. A gust of wind tore it away, starting fresh fires that claimed the lives of over 100,000 people.

5 47 Ronin Incident

In 1701, Lord Asano was ordered to commit ritual suicide for drawing his sword at court. His retainers, who had become *ronin*, or masterless samurai, avenged Asano's death by putting to death his opponent, Lord Kira, and placing his decapitated head on their master's grave. The act led the authorities to order the 47 loyal retainers to commit suicide.

6 Perry's "Black Ships"

On July 8, 1853, Commodore Matthew Calbraith Perry sailed four heavily armed ships into Edo Bay, to open Japan to diplomatic and trade relations. The "black ships" were a display of superior Western technology, a reminder of the astonishing progress that had bypassed the country.

Lithograph of Perry's "black ships"

7 Great Kanto Earthquake

At 11:58am on September 1, 1923, as people prepared lunch on charcoal braziers and gas burners, an earthquake measuring 7.9 on the Richter scale convulsed the city. Over 140,000 people were crushed or burned to death, and 45 percent of the buildings were destroyed. This horrific event obliterated many traces of the past.

8 Tokyo Air Raids

US raids on Tokyo during World War II exacted a heavy toll on civilian lives. Tokyo suffered 102 raids in all, the worst on the night of March 9–10, 1945, when over 300 B-29 bombers, loaded with oil, jellied gasoline, and napalm, swooped over tightly packed residential areas to the east, killing between 80,000 and 100,000 civilians.

Pole vault, 1964 Tokyo Olympics

9 1964 Tokyo Olympics

The first games to be held in Asia and telecast live overseas, the summer Olympics of 1964 saw the city reborn from the ashes of World War II, with modern stadiums, an expressway, and the start of the Shinkansen bullet train services.

10 Aum Shinrikyo Subway Attack

On March 20, 1995, members of the death cult movement Aum Shinrikyo, under orders from their leader, Shoko Asahara, placed plastic bags containing liquid sarin gas on the carriage floors on five subway lines. This act of domestic terrorism, the worst in modern Japanese history, killed 12 passengers and hundreds more were injured.

TOP 10 FAMOUS TOKYOITES

Great Wave **by Katsushika Hokusai**

1 Katsushika Hokusai
A famous woodblock artist of the Edo period, Hokusai (1760–1849) published 30,000 sketches and 500 books.

2 Soseki Natsume
Regarded by many as Japan's greatest writer, Natsume (1867–1916) set several of his novels in Tokyo.

3 Ichiyo Higuchi
The face of the writer Higuchi (1872–96), who died from tuberculosis, graces the ¥5,000 Japanese note.

4 Kafu Nagai
A fine chronicler of the Tokyo demimonde, Nagai (1879–1959) traced the transformation of the city.

5 Junichiro Tanizaki
Tanizaki (1886–1965) explored themes of sexuality, Western modernity, and materialism in his novels.

6 Yasujiro Ozu
Legendary film director Ozu (1903–63) described the collapse of the traditional Japanese family in *Tokyo Story*.

7 Akira Kurosawa
Kurosawa (1910–98), Japan's best-known film auteur, inspired Steven Spielberg and George Lucas.

8 Yoko Ono
Ono (b. 1933) was a reputed artist, musician, and experimental filmmaker long before she met John Lennon.

9 Hayao Miyazaki
Miyazaki (b. 1941) is the Oscar-winning director of *Spirited Away* and many other classics of Japanese animation.

10 Ryuichi Sakamoto
Sakamoto (b. 1952), a prolific composer, wrote the music for Bernardo Bertolucci's Oscar-winning film, *The Last Emperor*.

Historic Buildings

1 Hongan-ji Temple
MAP N5 ▪ 3-15-1 Tsukiji, Chuo-ku ▪ 3541-1131

Even in a city known for its architectural hybrids, this temple, inspired by Indian architecture, is extraordinary. Its designer, Chuta Ito, traveled all over Asia, and paid homage to the Indian origins of Buddhism in this 1935 building.

Imposing facade of Hongan-ji Temple

2 National Diet Building
MAP K4 ▪ 1-7-1 Nagatacho, Chiyoda-ku ▪ 5521-7445 ▪ Open 8am–5pm Mon–Fri ▪ Closed public holidays

Home to the Japanese Diet, or parliament, this building was completed in 1936. It has a pyramid-shaped dome and is divided into two main chambers – the Lower and Upper Houses. Weekday tours include the Public Gallery, Emperor's Room, and Central Hall, with its floor mosaic of a million pieces of marble.

3 Crafts Gallery
The finely finished Meiji-era structure, which houses the Crafts Gallery *(see p76)*, originally served as the headquarters of the Imperial Guard. Built in a style that came to be known as "19th-century Renaissance," it is one of the few protected buildings in a city notorious for its weak preservation ethic.

4 Kyu Iwasaki-tei Mansion
MAP F2 ▪ 1-3-45 Ikenohata, Taito-ku ▪ 3823-8340 ▪ Open 9am–5pm ▪ Adm

A fine example of Meiji-era syncreticism, this grand 1896 wooden residence was built by English architect Josiah Conder in a mix of Jacobean, Gothic, and Pennsylvanian country styles. Original features include coffered wood ceilings, stone fireplaces, parquet flooring, and Japan's first Western-style toilet.

5 Bank of Japan
The bank's *(see p75)* solid Neo-Classical outline was designed by Kingo Tatsuno, Japan's first Western-style architect. The 1896 building stands on the old site of the shogunate's former mint. A guided tour in English introduces the structure, its history, and present-day function.

Chamber of the National Diet Building

A splendid cupola adorns Tokyo Station's main hall

6 Tokyo Station

Threatened with demolition on many occasions, the Tokyo Station building *(see p76)* has survived thanks to the efforts of preservation groups over the years. Its future now seems assured. Designed by Kingo Tatsuno, the 1914 structure is faced with locally made bricks and reinforced with steel shipped from Britain and the United States.

7 Gokoku-ji Temple

MAP C1 ■ 5-40-1 Otsuka, Bunkyo-ku ■ 3941-0764

The temple grounds have interesting features, including a belfry and a rare two-story pagoda. The main hall, with its colossal wooden pillars, massive copper roof, and dark interior full of priceless Buddhist artifacts, is the centerpiece of this grand complex.

8 Hattori Building

MAP M4 ■ 4-5-11 Ginza, Chuo-ku ■ 3562-2111 ■ Open 10:30am–7pm

Commonly known as the Wako Building, this 1932 structure, created by Jin Watanabe, is a Ginza landmark. Named after the jeweler it houses, the building has appeared as a backdrop in several old movies. The interior is just as impressive as the exterior.

9 Ministry of Justice Building

MAP L4 ■ 1-1-1 Kasumigaseki, Chiyoda-ku ■ 3580-4111

Although not open to the public, the building's exterior, well renovated in the 1990s, is worth a look. A German company, Ende and Böckmann, designed this 1895 redbrick structure in a style that mixes formal elegance with functionality.

10 Nikolai Cathedral

The 1891 cathedral *(see p43)* was lucky to survive the 1923 earthquake, with only its onion domes destroyed. A new green dome was placed on top of the cruciform Russian Orthodox church after the disaster, and impressive stained-glass windows were installed.

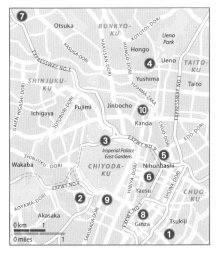

TOP 10 Places of Worship

1 Senso-ji Temple

This massive religious edifice (*see pp14–15*) is the focus of life in the Asakusa district. The sweeping roof of the main hall is visible from Kaminari-mon, the great gate to the temple. Inside the main hall, burning candles, incense sticks, and votive plaques add to the air of sanctity.

Richly decorated Senso-ji Temple

2 Sengaku-ji Temple

MAP C1 ▪ 2-11-1 Takanawa, Minato-ku ▪ 3441-5560 ▪ Open 7am–6pm (to 5pm Oct–Mar)

The tombs of the 47 loyal *ronin* (retainers), who committed suicide after avenging their master's death (*see p38*), can be found in this temple, which dates from 1612. The main hall was obliterated in the 1945 air raids but has been faithfully reconstructed.

3 Kanda Myojin Shrine

MAP F3 ▪ 2-16-2 Soto-Kanda, Chiyoda-ku ▪ 3254-0753

Founded in 730, but first built on this site in 1616, this temple has been rebuilt many times. The current reconstruction of the 1616 design, has a copper roof, copper *torii* gate, and an ornate main entrance gate.

4 Nezu Shrine

MAP E1 ▪ 1-28-9 Nezu, Bunkyo-ku ▪ 3822-0753

Established in 1706 by the fifth shogun, Tsunayoshi, Nezu Shrine is dedicated to Inari, the goddess of rice. The shrine grounds have retained most of the original structures. Tall cedars, ginkgo trees, and a carp pond create a strikingly natural setting. A painted gate, orange *torii* (gates), and bright banners add color.

5 Yushima Seido Temple

MAP F3 ▪ 1-4-25 Yushima, Bunkyo-ku ▪ 3251-4606 ▪ Open 9:30am–5pm (to 4pm Oct–Mar)

One of the few Confucian temples in Tokyo, Yushima Seido was founded in 1632. The current site and its great stone-flagged courtyard date from 1935. A statue of Confucius is located near the main gate.

6 Yasukuni Shrine

MAP D3 ▪ 3-1-1 Kudankita, Chiyoda-ku ▪ 3261-8326 ▪ Open 9am–4:30pm

Politics and religion coexist uncomfortably at Yasukuni Shrine, dedicated to the souls of Japan's war

Entrance to Kanda Myojin Shrine

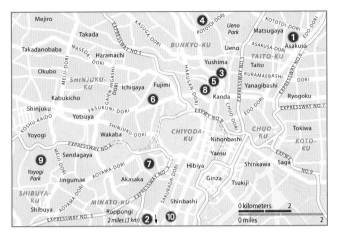

dead. Built in 1869, the shrine has some interesting features including an imposing *torii* gate, cherry trees, a pond-garden, and teahouse.

7 Hie Shrine

Reconstructed in 1958 after the Tokyo air raids, the 1659 building originally served as the protective shrine of Edo Castle. In gratitude, successive shoguns donated lavish gifts of swords and sacred horses to the shrine *(see p95)*. A line of orange *torii* gates forms a colorful tunnel through the grounds.

8 Nikolai Cathedral

MAP F3 ■ 4-1 Kanda-Surugadai, Chiyoda-ku ■ 3295-6879 ■ Open 1–4pm (to 3:30pm Oct–Mar)

Built with funds provided by a Russian czar and designed by English architect Josiah Conder, this late 19th-century Russian Orthodox church is an interesting anomaly among the temples and shrines of the city. It was named after its founder St. Nikolai Kassatkin, a 19th-century missionary who converted thousands of Japanese in the northern island of Hokkaido.

9 Meiji Shrine

Dedicated to the souls of Emperor Meiji and his consort Empress Shoken, this impressive shrine *(see pp30–31)* was built in the pure Shinto architectural style. This is reflected in everything from its gravel forecourt, cypress pillars, and the clean lines of the main hall to the copper roof that floats majestically above it all.

A 1970s reconstruction, Zojo-ji

10 Zojo-ji Temple

The venue for the funerals of six Tokugawa shoguns, this temple *(see p97)* is best visited for its main gate, Sangedatsu-mon, which dates from 1605, and Daibonsho, a 15-tonne bell. There's also a Himalayan cedar planted by former US president Ulysses S. Grant in 1879.

⏱10 Museums

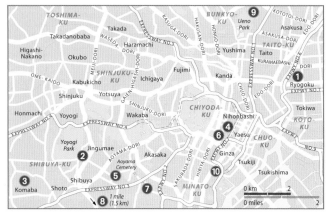

1 Edo-Tokyo Museum

This fabulous museum (see pp18–19) traces the history of Edo and Tokyo, charting its growth from a fishing village to today's megacity. Displays and models cover both the creation of the city and the natural and man-made disasters that have reshaped it.

Model displayed Edo-Tokyo Museum

2 Ota Memorial Museum of Art

This fascinating museum's (see p101) extensive private collection of *ukiyo-e* woodblock prints is constantly displayed in new exhibitions. The images present a colorful cross-section of life in the city of Edo, from its streets and fish markets to the pleasure quarters.

3 Japan Folk Crafts Museum

MAP C1 ▪ 4-3-33 Komaba, Meguro-ku ▪ 3467-4527 ▪ Open 10am–5pm Tue–Sun ▪ Adm ▪ www.mingeikan.or.jp

This museum displays a large collection of woodwork, ceramic ware, textiles, metal, glass work, and furniture created by largely anonymous artists from Japan, China, Korea, and Taiwan.

4 Intermediatheque

On the second and third floors of the Kitte shopping mall, resembling more of a high-design boutique than a traditional museum, Intermediatheque (see p76) displays eclectic items from the collection of the University of Tokyo. Cabinets of curiosities sit alongside contemporary installations and art. Adding to the quirkiness, gramophone record concerts are occasionally held for music lovers.

5 Nezu Museum

In an elegant building designed by Kengo Kuma, this art museum (see p100) displays treasures from Japan and East Asia in changing exhibitions. Its ornamental gardens feature bronze sculptures and a contemporary-style teahouse.

Exhibit at Idemitsu Museum of Arts

6 Idemitsu Museum of Arts

Housing one of the finest private collections of Japanese and Asian art in Tokyo, this museum *(see p82)* regularly rotates its exquisite Chinese, Korean, and Japanese ceramic ware and ancient pottery shards, calligraphy, and gold-painted screens. The collection includes over 15,000 items.

7 Mori Art Museum

MAP T5 ■ 6-10-1 Roppongi, Minato-ku ■ 5777-8600 ■ Open 10am–10pm Wed–Mon (to 5pm Tue) ■ Adm ■ www.mori.art.museum

There's no permanent collection here, but the enormous gallery spaces atop Roppongi Hills' Mori Tower regularly host some of Tokyo's biggest blockbuster art shows, with the likes of Takashi Murakami regularly showing.

Archeological relic, Tokyo National Museum

8 Tokyo Photographic Art Museum

MAP C1 ■ Ebisu Garden Place, 1-13-3 Mita, Meguro-ku ■ 3280-0099 ■ Open 10am–6pm Mon–Sun (to 8pm Thu & Fri) ■ Adm (only for special shows) ■ www.syabi.com

The big names in Japanese and Western photography are shown at this premier photography and video art space. Five floors follow the history of photography, displaying 30,000 images and photo-related items. Special exhibitions, featuring some of the world's best photographic work, run through the year.

9 Tokyo National Museum

This huge museum offers the world's largest collection of Japanese art and antiquity. Permanent Japanese exhibits are displayed in the Honkan; archeological relics in the Heiseikan; Chinese, Korean, and Central Asian arts in the Toyokan; and Buddhist sculpture and scrolls in the Gallery of Horyu-ji Treasures *(see pp24–7)*.

10 Ad Museum Tokyo

The highly creative ad work on display at this fascinating venue *(see p83)* is sponsored by Dentsu, Japan's largest advertising operation. Permanent exhibits explore the long history of commercial art in Japan. A TV room makes it possible to view excellent commercials.

Creative exhibition at the Mori Art Museum in Tokyo

Art Galleries

1 Spiral
MAP B6 ■ 5-6-23 Minami-Aoyama, Minato-ku ■ 3498-1171 ■ Open 8am–11pm

Designed by leading architect Fumihiko Maki, this gallery presents art, music, film, and theater. A spiral ramp above a first-floor café leads visitors into the main gallery spaces.

2 Shiseido Gallery
MAP M5 ■ Tokyo Ginza Shiseido Bldg B1, 8-8-3 Ginza, Chuo-ku ■ 3572-3901 ■ Open 11am–7pm Tue–Sat (to 6pm Sun) ■ www.shiseidogroup.jp/gallery

The chic Shiseido Gallery features contemporary Japanese and international artists, retrospectives, and fashion-linked exhibitions.

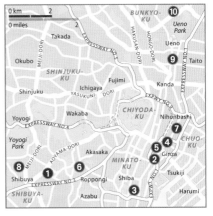

Striking Shiseido Gallery

3 The Tolman Collection
MAP E6 ■ 2-2-18 Shiba Daimon, Minato-ku ■ 3434-1300 ■ Open 11am–7pm Wed–Sun ■ www.tolmantokyo.com

This gallery has more than 2,000 contemporary Japanese prints, aquatints, etchings, lithographs, and woodblocks. Signed and numbered editions of work by artists such as Shingo Araki and Miki Gojo are also included.

4 Gallery Koyanagi
MAP N4 ■ 1-7-5 Ginza, Chuo-ku ■ 3561-1896 ■ Open 11am–7pm Tue–Sat ■ www.gallery koyanagi.com

Leading Japanese and international photo and print artists showcase their works in this spacious commercial gallery tucked away on the eighth floor of an office building.

5 Ginza Graphic Gallery
MAP M5 ■ DNP Ginza Bldg, 1F, 7-7-2 Ginza, Chuo-ku ■ 3571-5206 ■ Open 11am–7pm Mon–Fri (to 6pm Sat) ■ www.dnp.co.jp/gallery/ggg_e

Reopened April 2016 following restoration, the Ginza is sponsored by DNP, one of Japan's largest printing outfits. The gallery features work by Japanese graphic designers.

Dramatic glass building housing the National Art Center, Tokyo

6 National Art Center, Tokyo

Covering 516,668 sq ft (48,000 sq m), this massive space for art *(see p95)* comprises 12 exhibition rooms that host a variety of shows curated by NACT as well as by art associations from across Japan.

7 Zeit-Foto Salon

MAP N4 ■ Kyoei Bldg 1F, 3-5-3 Kyobashi, Chuo-ku ■ 3535-7188 ■ Open 10:30am–6:30pm Tue–Fri (to 5:30pm Sat) ■ www.zeit-foto.com

This is one of the oldest photo galleries in Tokyo, with a huge collection of images encompassing 19th-century prints and the work of 20th-century masters in the field, such as Man Ray and Lee Friedlander. Controversial Japanese artists, including photographer Ryoko Suzuki, and big international names ensure that the shows are always stimulating.

8 Tokyo Wonder Site

MAP Q5 ■ 1-19-8 Jinnan, Shibuya-ku ■ 3463-0603 ■ Open 11am–7pm Tue–Sun ■ www.tokyo-ws.org

A Tokyo Metropolitan Government-run operation, Tokyo Wonder Site aims to promote new, emerging artists and cultural events. With exhibitions on its three floors turning over at a rapid pace, this gallery represents a thriving art scene.

9 3331 Arts Chiyoda

MAP F2 ■ 6-11-14 Sotokanda, Chiyoda-ku ■ 6803-2441 ■ Open noon–7pm Wed–Mon ■ www.3331.jp

A short stroll from the anime, manga, and computer-geek nexus of Akihabara, the exhibitions, interactive installations, and art workshops in this former school are guaranteed to be fun and eclectic.

Art workshop, 3331 Arts Chiyoda

10 SCAI – The Bathhouse

MAP F1 ■ Kashiwayu-Ato, 6-1-23 Yanaka, Taito-ku ■ 3821-1144 ■ Open noon–6pm Tue–Sat ■ www.scaithebathhouse.com

This gallery is located in a converted Edo-period bathhouse in the endearing old district of Yanaka. It showcases well-known experimental Japanese artists and introduces foreign artists.

TOP10 Modern and Contemporary Buildings

Mode Gakuen Cocoon Tower

1 Mode Gakuen Cocoon Tower

MAP U2 ■ 1-7-3 Nishi-Shinjuku, Shinjuku-ku

One of the slickest high rises to adorn Tokyo's cityscape, this 2008 building in Shinjuku was designed by Kenzo Tange Associates. Its criss-cross exterior pattern, rising up 50 floors, takes inspiration from a silkworm cocoon.

2 Nakagin Capsule Tower

MAP M5 ■ 8-16-10 Ginza, Chuo-ku

Kisho Kurokawa (1934–2007) was one of the founders of what became known as the Metabolist movement in architecture. His seminal Tokyo building is the Nakagin Capsule Tower from 1972, made out of 140 interchangeable concrete "pods."

3 Asahi Beer Hall

MAP S3 ■ 1-23-1 Azuma-bashi, Sumida-ku

The 1989 building was designed by Philippe Starck. It's also known as Super Dry Hall and *Flamme d'Or*, after the giant golden sculpture on its roof, which is meant to symbolize the frothy head of the brewing company's beer.

4 Tokyo Metropolitan Government Building

Stand back in the semicircular Citizen's Plaza, at the foot of the Tokyo Metropolitan Government Building *(see p109)*, to fully admire the symmetry of Kenzo Tange's 48-story, twin-towered creation. It cleverly channels Paris's Notre-Dame Cathedral via a very 20th-century Japanese prism.

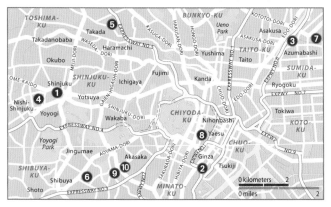

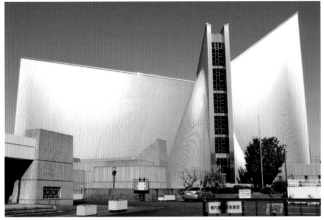

Stylish exterior of St. Mary's Cathedral

⑤ St. Mary's Cathedral
MAP C1 ■ 3-16-15 Sekiguchi, Bunkyo-ku ■ 3945-0126

After the original Gothic Catholic cathedral here burned down during World War II, it was redesigned in 1964 by Kenzo Tange, who was also the architect responsible for the Olympic Stadium at Yoyogi.

⑥ Prada Aoyama Building
Swiss architects Herzog & de Meuron made a splash on the designer-shopping avenue Omotesando in 2003 with this six-story contemporary boutique *(see p104)* for the famous Italian fashion house. Covered in rhomboid-shaped green-glass windows, it looks like it has been bubble-wrapped.

⑦ Tokyo Skytree
Hard to ignore, Tokyo Skytree *(see p89)* is the world's tallest free-standing tower, visible from many parts of the city. For all its modernity, it is built along similar principles to those

Tokyo Skytree looming high above the city

used by architects for centuries in order to protect temple pagodas against earthquakes.

⑧ Tokyo International Forum
Rafael Viñoly's 1996 construction *(see p82)* is symbolic of the end of 20th-century architecture in Tokyo. The construction is made up of several performance halls and a convention center hanging off an elliptical enclosure made of nearly 3,000 panels of tempered glass.

⑨ National Art Center, Tokyo
Kisho Kurokawa's final hurrah is this 2007 exhibition space *(see p95)* forming one point of the Roppongi Art Triangle. The undulating glass-and-steel facade is amazing, but even better is the soaring lobby dominated by two giant inverted cones.

⑩ 21_21 Design Sight
MAP D5 ■ 9-7-6 Akasaka, Minato-ku ■ 3475-2121 ■ www. 2121designsight.jp

Like an iceberg, Tadao Ando's 21_21 Design Site is mainly underground with its presence announced only by the sharp-edge steel plate roofs of two low pavilions. The exhibition halls are made from polished concrete.

🔟 Gardens and Parks

from 1654. Standing near the garden entrance is a large black pine, planted in 1704, a miraculous survivor of earthquakes, fires, and air raids. The most interesting feature of this large garden is a tidal pond that brings in saltwater fish.

3 Hibiya Park

Part of a feudal estate converted into a military parade ground, Hibiya Park *(see p81)* was Japan's first Western-style park when it opened in 1903. A lawn, rose garden, bandstand, and theater occupy the center of the park. A pond, with its original fountain in the shape of a heron, and a giant wisteria trellis are tucked away in the western corner.

4 Mukojima Hyakka-en Garden

MAP D1 ■ 3-18-3 Higashi-Mukojima, Sumida-ku ■ 3611-8705 ■ Open 9am–5pm ■ Adm

This little-visited Edo-period garden was completed in 1804 close to Sumida River *(see pp16–17)*, a district of temples and teahouses serving as the focal point for a refined social and cultural life.

5 Kiyosumi-teien Garden

MAP H4 ■ 3-3-9 Kiyosumi, Koto-ku ■ 3641-5892 ■ Open 9am–5pm ■ Adm

Rare rocks were shipped from all over the country in steam ships to create this garden, which was once part of an estate owned by a rich timber merchant. A traditional teahouse overlooks a large pond and islets, where you can spot fish and turtles. Another eye-catching feature is an artificial hill, shaped into the likeness of Mount Fuji.

1 Canadian Embassy Garden

MAP C5 ■ Canadian Embassy 4F, 7-3-38 Akasaka, Minato-ku ■ 5412-6200 ■ Open 9:30am–5:30pm Mon–Fri

Built across an upper terrace of the building, this stone garden was created by Masuno Shunmyo, one of the most innovative garden designers working in Japan today. The stone garden symbolizes, through the use of stones brought from Hiroshima to represent the ancient rocks that form the Canadian Shield, the relationship between Japan and Canada.

2 Hama Rikyu Garden

An original Edo-period garden, Hama Rikyu *(see p82)* dates

Hama Rikyu Garden

Koishikawa Korakuen Garden

6 Koishikawa Korakuen Garden

Tokyo's oldest garden *(see pp28–9)* re-creates famous scenes in minia-ture from Japan and China. A simple grass-covered knoll represents Mount Lu in China's Jiangxi Province, while a shallow stream stands in for Oikawa River in Kyoto.

7 Shinjuku Gyoen

Excelling at variety, this garden *(see p107)* was completed in 1772. The current garden, a multicultural masterpiece, is divided into French, English, and Japanese sections. An old, domed botanical greenhouse holds tropical plants.

Spring blossom, Shinjuku Gyoen

8 Rikugi-en Garden

MAP C1 ■ 6-16-3 Hon-Komagome, Bunkyo-ku ■ 3941-2222 ■ Open 9am–5pm ■ Adm

Completed in 1702, this garden was named after the six principles used in the composition of Oriental poetry. While the garden's hidden symbolism is not easy to decipher, its curvaceous landscapes, simple Zen-style teahouses, and profusion of trees can be appreciated by all.

9 Yoyogi Park

MAP A5 ■ 2-1 Yoyogi-Kamizono cho, Shibuya-ku ■ 3469-6081 ■ Open daily

A wide open area of grassy lawns and recreational facilities popular with families, cyclists, joggers, and skateboarders, Yoyogi Park makes a great spot for an impromptu picnic. A small botanical garden and bird sanctuary add interest and live music concerts are held here every Sunday *(see p57)*. The park forms one of the largest forested areas of Tokyo.

10 Institute for Nature Study and Park

MAP C1 ■ 5-21-5 Shirokanedai, Minato-ku ■ 3441-7176 ■ Open May–Aug: 9am–5pm Tue–Sun; Sep–Apr: 9am–4:30pm ■ Adm

A carefully preserved section of the Musashino Plain, the Institute for Nature Study's park is home to a variety of birds, insects, and turtles in addition to 8,000-plus trees. A small museum at the entrance traces Tokyo's declining greenery.

Off the Beaten Path

Items for sale, Shimokitazawa

among the most pleasant areas of the city to browse trendy boutiques, convivial bars, and cafés. The cherry tree-lined Meguro River is also a prime viewing spot during *hanami* (cherry blossom) season.

 4 Kyu-Furukawa Gardens
MAP C1 ▪ 1-27-39 Nishigahara, Kita-ku ▪ 3910-0394 ▪ Open 9am–5pm

Rose beds and azalea bushes are a feature of Kyu-Furukawa Gardens. Admire them while sipping *matcha* (green tea) in the teahouse.

1 Shimokitazawa
MAP C1

Fashionable youth fill the warren of narrow streets southwest of Shibuya on weekends for clothing, thrift stores, music clubs, and small experimental theaters.

2 Ikebukuro
MAP C1

This northern district, set around a train station, offers mega department stores, Otome Road's manga and anime shops, and the Frank Lloyd Wright-designed school Myonichikan.

3 Daikanyama and Naka- Meguro
MAP C1

One stop southwest of Shibuya, Dainkanyama and Naka-Meguro are

Cherry tree-lined Meguro River

5 Toden Arakawa Streetcar Line

The last of Tokyo's city-operated streetcar lines still operates between Waseda and Minowabashi, arcing 7.5 miles (12 km) across the north of the city. It's a retro treat that costs just ¥170 and a relaxing insight into less touristy parts of Tokyo.

6 Tennozu Isle
MAP C2

East of Shinagawa, towards Tokyo Bay, Tennozu Isle came on the radar in the late 1990s, when one of its old waterside warehouses became the home of TY Harbor Brewery. The same company has since launched the area's bakery café, Breadworks. There are several commercial art galleries opening here, as well as street-art festivals being held.

7 Ningyocho
MAP G4

Between Nihonbashi and the Sumida River is this *shitamachi* (old town Tokyo) district of small temples, shrines, traditional shopping, and dining. Check out the craft stores along retail parade Amazake Yokocho.

8 Ryogoku
MAP G3 ■ National Sumo Stadium: 1-3-28 Yokoami, Sumida-ku; 3623-5111 ■ Museum: open 10am–4:30pm Mon–Fri ■ www.sumo.or.jp

Tournaments lasting 15 days are held at this neighborhood's National Sumo Stadium in January, May, and September; at other times of the year, the building has a small sumo museum. Ryogoku is also home to the fascinating Edo-Tokyo Museum (see pp18–19).

Sumo wrestlers prepare to compete

9 Japanese Sword Museum
MAP A4 ■ 4-25-10 Yoyogi, Shibuya-ku ■ 3379-1386 ■ Open 9:30am–5pm Tue–Sun ■ Adm ■ www.touken.or.jp

Over 30 of the 120 Japanese swords here are designated National Treasures and are arguably the finest instruments of death ever made.

10 Kagurazaka
MAP D3 ■ 1-10 Akagi-Motomachi, Shinjuku-ku ■ 3260-5071

Once a thriving geisha quarter, Kagurazaka's charming narrow cobbled streets, shops, and cafés evoke old-time Tokyo. The area's Akagi Shrine, however, received a contemporary makeover in 2010 by prominent architect Kengo Kuma.

TOP 10 HOT SPRINGS AND BATHS

Guests at Oedo Onsen Monogatari

1 Oedo Onsen Monogatari
MAP D2 ■ 2-6-3 Aomi, Koto-ku ■ 5500-1126
Hot-spring theme park in Odaiba.

2 Toshimaen Niwa no Yu
MAP C1 ■ 3-25-1 Koyama, Nerima-ku ■ 3990-4126
Spa with multiple zones, inside and out, including mixed bathing.

3 Komparu-yu
MAP M5 ■ 8-7-5 Ginza, Chuo-ku ■ 3571-5469
An old *sento* (ornate bathhouse).

4 Rokuryu Onsen
MAP F1 ■ 3-4-20 Ikenohata, Taito-ku ■ 3821-3826
A sento featuring amber-colored water.

5 Take no Yu
MAP D6 ■ 1-15-12 Minami-Azabu, Minato-ku ■ 3453-1446
Revamped *sento* not far from Roppongi.

6 Jakotsuyu
MAP R2 ■ 1-11-11 Asakusa, Taito-ku ■ 3841-8645
Spa with a Mount Fuji mural in the bathing hall.

7 Maenohara Onsen
MAP C1 ■ 3-41-1 Maenocho, Itabashi-ku ■ 5916-3826
An open-air hot spring.

8 Shimizu-yu
MAP C6 ■ 3-12-3 Minami-Aoyama, Minato-ku ■ 3401-4404
A sento just steps from Omotesando.

9 Spa LaQua
MAP E1 ■ Tokyo Dome City, 1-3-61 Koraku, Bunkyo-ku ■ 5800-9999
Fancy spa complex next to Tokyo Dome.

10 Kamata Onsen
MAP B2 ■ 2-23-2 Kamata-Honcho, Ota-ku ■ 3732-1126
A sento with retro-appeal.

TOP 10 Children's Attractions

1 Tokyo Sea Life Park
MAP B1 ■ 6-2-3 Rinkai-cho, Edogawa-ku ■ 3869-5152 ■ Open 9:30am–5pm Thu–Tue ■ Adm ■ www.tokyo-zoo.net/english/kasai/main.html

The highlight of this large aquarium, on the east side of Tokyo Bay, is the huge doughnut-shaped tank housing sharks, tuna, and a myriad of other species. There are also penguins, auks, and puffins here.

Underwater tank, Tokyo Sea Life Park

2 Drum Museum
MAP Q3 ■ 2-1-1 Nishi-Asakusa, Taito-ku ■ 3842-5622 ■ Open 10am–5pm Wed–Sun ■ Adm

This interactive museum has a collection of over 600 *taiko* (drums) from all over the world. The highlight are the Japanese festival drums. Skins with a blue sticker can be played, but with care, while those with a red mark cannot be touched. A stickerless drum can be played freely.

A vibrant display at the Kite Museum

3 Ghibli Museum
Hayao Miyazaki's animations, surreal landscapes, whimsical characters, and fanciful sets can be seen here *(see p116)*. Kid's will love the "wonderland" atmosphere.

4 KidZania
MAP G6 ■ Lalaport Toyosu, 2-4-9 Toyosu, Koto-ku ■ 0570-06-4012 ■ Open 9am–3pm, 4–9pm ■ Adm ■ www.kidzania.jp

Children under 12 can experience the working world of adults by role-playing in dozens of jobs, such as TV anchor, pizza chef, barber, banker and cop in a realistic city setting. They even get paid in "kidZos", the official currency of KidZania.

5 Ueno Zoo
MAP F1 ■ 9-83 Ueno Koen, Taito-ku ■ 3828-5171 ■ Open 9:30am–5pm Tue–Sun ■ Adm ■ www.tokyo-zoo.net/english/ueno

Japan's oldest zoo, built in 1882, Ueno Zoo is home to over 400 different species, including giant pandas, gorillas, Indian lions, apes, and Sumatran tigers. There is a monorail ride above the zoo to a children's animal petting zone.

6 Kite Museum
Displayed at this delightful museum *(see p77)* are around 3,000 kites, shaped variously as squid, sumo wrestlers, and Mount Fuji. Some are illustrated with the faces of manga characters, samurai warriors, and Kabuki actors.

7 National Museum of Nature and Science

The model of a giant whale greets visitors to this museum *(see p87)*, which has dinosaur displays, exhibits on botany, fossils, asteroids, and ocean ography, among other attractions.

8 Tokyo Disney Resort®

Mickey and pals will pull out all the stops for kids (and adults) in this fantasyland *(see p116)* of castles, magic mountains, haunted mansions, Polynesian villages, and steamboat rides.

9 Tokyo Dome City

MAP E2 ■ 1-3-61 Koraku, Bunkyo-ku ■ 5800-9999 ■ Open 10am–9pm ■ Adm ■ www.tokyo-dome.co.jp/e

This amusement park has a free-fall parachute ride, Sky Flower, but the highlight is the rollercoaster Thunder Dolphin. LaQua, the park's other section, features a selection of eateries, shops, and spas.

Ferris wheel, Tokyo Dome City

10 National Museum of Emerging Science and Innovation

Known more simply as Miraikan, this fascinating museum *(see p35)* in Odaiba is packed with hands-on attractions to entertain and educate both adults and kids. The exhibits have excellent English translations. The museum's star attraction is a demonstration by Asimo, the walking robot.

TOP 10 SHOPS FOR KIDS

Kiddy Land, set over five floors

1 Kiddy Land
MAP S4 ■ 6-1-9 Jingumae, Shibuya-ku ■ 3409-3431
Store filled with cuddly character models and games.

2 Crayon House
MAP C5 ■ 3-8-15 Kita-Aoyama, Minato-ku ■ 3406-6308
A family center with toys and books.

3 Hakuhinkan Toy Park
MAP M5 ■ 8-8-11 Ginza, Chuo-ku ■ 3571-8008
The latest models, characters, and games plus some great restaurants.

4 BorneLund
MAP S4 ■ 1-3-12 Jingumae, Shibuya-ku ■ 5411-8022
Good-quality imported toys.

5 Yamashiroya Toy Shop
MAP F2 ■ 6-14-6 Ueno, Taito-ku ■ 3831-2320
A six-floor shop stuffed with toys.

6 Tsukumo Robot Kingdom
MAP F3 ■ 1-9-7 Soto-Kanda, Chiyoda-ku ■ 3251-0987
Specialists in small robotic animals.

7 Aso Bit City
MAP F3 ■ 1-15-18 Soto-Kanda, Chiyoda-ku ■ 5298-3581
Fun electronic goods, train sets, and manga characters.

8 Sayegusa
MAP M4 ■ 4-4-4 Ginza, Chuo-ku ■ 3573-2441
Children's clothes and accessories.

9 Pokémon Center Mega Tokyo
The best merchandise of the "Pocket Monsters" anime series *(see p56)*.

10 Kuramae–Asakusabashi Toy Street
MAP G3 ■ Kuramae, Taito-ku
Wholesalers showcase their wares along this traditional toy street.

TOP 10 Pop Culture Venues

Performers dressed as robots entertain customers in Robot Restaurant

1 Robot Restaurant
MAP B3 ■ 1-7-1 Kabukicho, Shinjuku-ku ■ 3200-5500 ■ Open 4pm–11pm ■ www.shinjuku-robot.com

The lively crowd don't come here for the food, but for the over-the-top performance by robots and outrageously dressed girls and guys bathed in a sea of flashing lights.

2 Takeshita-dori
MAP B5 ■ Takeshita-dori, Shibuya-ku

Packed with garish boutiques, subculture junk, cutesy accessories, lurid kitsch, and fetish costumery, this loud, abrasive but fun street is frequented by Japan's extreme youth.

3 Design Festa Gallery
MAP R4 ■ 3-20-18 Jingumae, Shibuya-ku ■ 3479-1442 ■ www.designfesta.com/en

The Design Festa event encourages freedom of expression through art and design and has been held twice a year since 1994. This gallery, run by the organizers of the event, is open for temporary exhibitions all year round.

4 Pokémon Center Mega Tokyo
MAP C1 ■ Sunshine City Alpha 2F, 3-1-2 Higashi-Ikebukuro, Toshima-ku ■ 5927-9290 ■ Open 10am–8pm ■ www.pokemon.co.jp

This is the biggest of several stores in Tokyo selling Pokémon-related merchandise. Expect to find no end of themed clothes, figures, toys, and snacks as well as Pokémon statues.

5 Tokyo Anime Center
MAP F3 ■ DNP Ichigaya-tamachi Bldg, 1-14-1 Ichigaya-tamachi, Shinjuku-ku ■ 3170-0903 ■ Open 11am–8pm Tue–Sun ■ www.animecenter.jp

Formerly located in bustling Akihabara, the center caters to die-hard anime fans and features temporary as well as permanent exhibitions showcasing anime-production techniques.

6 Tokyo Big Sight
MAP D2 ■ Tokyo International Exhibition Center, 3-11-1 Ariake, Koto-ku ■ 5530-1111

Arguably Asia's largest art festival, the biannual, two-day Design Festa (see p70) is held at Tokyo Big Sight and attracts over 50,000 visitors.

Tokyo Big Sight, home to Design Festa

7 Ghibli Museum

Make sure you book ahead to visit this popular and charming museum *(see p116)*, which brings to life the characters and fantasy environments of the animated movies created by Hayao Miyazaki and his colleagues at Studio Ghibli.

8 Sunday in the Park

Tokyo's theater of dress spills over from busy Harajuku into Yoyogi Park *(see p51)* every Sunday, where you may chance upon costumes reflecting every trend since the 1950s. Live bands set up during the afternoon along the sidewalk between the park and Olympic pavilions.

9 Center Gai

MAP B6 ■ Shibuya, Shibuya-ku

A bustling pedestrian street crammed with inexpensive bars, cafés, and restaurants as well as stores selling music records, cell phones, clothes, and jewelry. Center Gai is the epicenter of Japanese youth culture – full of teens and early twentysomethings.

Shoppers thronging Center Gai

10 Nakano Broadway

MAP C1 ■ 5-52-15 Nakano, Nakano-ku ■ 3388-7004 ■ Open noon–8pm, some stores may vary

A smaller and less frantic version of Tokyo's *otaku* mecca, Akihabara, Nakano Broadway is anime and manga heaven. The complex is a short walk from Nakano Station, packed with stores selling everything from comics to game consoles to collectible figurines.

TOP 10 CULTURAL PHENOMENA

Hello Kitty attraction

1 Hello Kitty
Launched in 1974, this helplessly naive but adorable creature has a button nose and, inexplicably, no mouth.

2 Cosplay
Cosu-pure, or costume play, refers to cross-dressing in outfits worn mainly by manga or anime characters.

3 Capsule Hotels
Architect Kisho Kurokawa's 1972 Nakagin Capsule Building inspired the idea of the capsule hotel.

4 Maid Cafés
Young women in white tights, pink hair, lace caps, and aprons respectfully serve tea and cakes.

5 Purikura
These photo booths provide instant digital photos that can be enhanced with all manner of designs to create manga-style selfies.

6 Manga Kissa
For a cup of coffee at a *kissa*, short for *kissaten* (café), manga fans can access hundreds of comic books.

7 Hip Fashion Minorities
Harajuku and Shibuya are full of cyber-punks and "Gothic Lolita" – girls in black makeup and Victorian frills.

8 Otaku
Otaku – geeks or nerds – are passionate about anime, manga, video games, and cute female star merchandise.

9 Love Hotels
There are over 20,000 short-stay love hotels in Tokyo alone, which feature various fantasy themes.

10 Pachinko
Pachinko, or Japanese pinball, is considered lowbrow, but there are parlors on most shopping streets.

ⓣⓞⓟ🔟 **Entertainment Venues**

Performance of *The Rose of Versailles* at Takarazuka Theater

① Takarazuka Theater
MAP M4 ▪ 1-1-3 Yurakucho, Chiyoda-ku ▪ 5251-2001 ▪ www.kageki.hankyu.co.jp

Established in 1914, the Takarazuka stages sentimental plays featuring an all-female cast, unlike Kabuki, which is an all-male preserve. *The Rose of Versailles*, with its rich costumes and dashing heroes, is a favorite. Synopses are provided in English.

② National Theatre
MAP D4 ▪ 4-1 Hayabusa-cho, Chiyoda-ku ▪ 3265-7411 ▪ www.ntj.jac.go.jp

The two stages at this performing arts complex regularly stage a variety of traditional entertainment, including Kabuki, Bunraku (puppetry), court music, and dance. English language earphone guides are available.

③ New National Theatre
MAP A4 ▪ 1-1-1 Honmachi, Shibuya-ku ▪ 5351-3011

The three stages – Playhouse, Opera House, and the Pit – cater to different audiences. Interpretations of Western classics by cutting-edge Japanese directors are highly regarded, though most foreign visitors prefer the more visual events like modern dance.

④ Bunkamura Theatre Cocoon
MAP A6 ▪ 2-24-1 Dogenzaka, Shibuya-ku ▪ 3477-9111

Housed in the huge Bunkamura culture and arts center, the Cocoon hosts concerts, musicals, and opera. A medium-sized theater, it is best known for performances of contemporary dance, ballet, and its long involvement with flamenco dance and music troupes from Spain.

⑤ National Noh Theatre
MAP B4 ▪ 4-18-1 Sendagaya, Shibuya-ku ▪ 3423-1331 ▪ www.ntj.jac.go.jp

The traditional performing art of Noh, based on ancient tales of avenging spirits and wandering ghosts, is very abstract to modern audiences, more like contemporary dance than a play. Read the English leaflet provided to make sense of the plot.

Musicians at a concert in Suntory Hall

⑥ Suntory Hall
MAP D5 ▪ 1-13-1 Akasaka, Minato-ku ▪ 3505-1001 ▪ www.suntory.co.jp/suntoryhall

Suntory Hall is said to have the best acoustics in Tokyo. This classical music concert hall sees top local and international performers gracing its stage. Once a month, it holds a free pipe organ recital during lunchtime.

⑦ Asakusa Engei Hall
MAP R2 ■ 1-43-12 Asakusa, Taito-ku ■ 3841-6545

Traditional comic storytelling takes place here. The seated narrators perform alone, with the barest of props, usually just a fan. Although it is exceedingly difficult for foreigners to follow, it is worth a visit for the atmosphere at least.

A show at Kabukiza Theatre

⑧ Kabukiza Theatre
Reconstructed in 2013, this Baroque Japanese revivalist-style building *(see p81)* stages Kabuki shows. Full dramas of three to four acts can extend throughout an afternoon or evening. Single-act tickets provide a shorter, more accessible entrée into Kabuki for the first timer.

⑨ Shinbashi Enbujo
MAP N5 ■ 6-18-2 Ginza, Chuo-ku ■ 3541-2600

This theater stages period dramas, whose plots are strong on the conflict between love and duty. "Super Kabuki," a modern dramatic form devised by veteran actor Ennosuke Ichikawa, guarantees to keep even non-Japanese audience members alert.

⑩ Tokyo Dome
MAP E2 ■ 1-3-61 Koraku, Bunkyo-ku ■ www.tokyo-dome.co.jp/e

Known locally by its nickname as the "Big Egg," this central Tokyo stadium is the home of top baseball team Yomiuri Giants; attending a game during the season is great fun. The venue is also used for pop concerts.

TOP 10 MOVIES SET IN TOKYO

1 Stray Dog (1949)
A rare chance to see what Tokyo's downtown streets looked like in the post-war era.

2 Tokyo Story (1953)
Yasujiro Ozu's classic, set mostly in a working-class area of the city, explores the collapse of the Japanese family.

3 Godzilla (1954)
Awakened by the A-bomb, the giant lizard stumbles through the city until pacified by Japanese scientists.

4 Diary of a Shinjuku Thief (1968)
Nagisa Oshima's film explores the minds of young Japanese radicals in this audacious film.

5 Shall We Dance? (1996)
Tokyo night scenes form the backdrop to this story of a salaryman who finds a higher purpose in ballroom dancing.

6 Lost in Translation (2003)
A fine performance from Bill Murray, but Sofia Coppola's stereotypical view of Tokyo is oddly dated.

7 Tokyo Godfathers (2003)
An animated classic that traces a tale of redemption for three tramps and the baby they discover in a trash can.

8 Babel (2006)
Oscar-nominated Rinko Kikuchi plays the mute Chieko in the Tokyo strand of this globetrotting movie.

9 Tokyo Sonata (2008)
How a middle-class Tokyo family reacts when the father loses his job and tries to keep it a secret.

10 Tokyo Tribe (2014)
Yakuza gang violence, martial arts action, and hip-hop music all collide in this fast-paced fantasy set in a divided Tokyo of the future.

Scene from *Tokyo Godfathers*

Clubs

1 Shinjuku Pit Inn
One of the oldest jazz clubs in Tokyo, this medium-sized venue's *(see p110)* musical tastes tend toward fusion and new direction jazz. Traditional bands also get an airing. Local and international acts perform here. One drink is included in the entry fee.

Jazz musician, Shinjuku Pit Inn

2 SuperDeluxe
As well as live music gigs by some of Tokyo's less mainstream singers and bands, this long-running events space *(see p98)* is also known for its PechaKucha evenings, where talks are given in a 20-slide format, shown for 20 seconds each.

3 Sound Museum Vision
MAP B6 ■ 2-10-7 Dogenzaka, Shibuya-ku ■ 5728-2824 ■ Adm ■ www.vision-tokyo.com
This huge labyrinthine club in a basement has a very impressive sound system, delivering mainly techno, house, and hip-hop music. The place is divided into different rooms for different moods. It also hosts theme nights frequently.

4 Club Quattro
MAP B6 ■ 32-13-4 Udagawacho, Shibuya-ku ■ 3477-8750 ■ See website for schedule ■ Adm ■ www.club-quattro.com/shibuya
This intimate venue has been going strong for decades now, and during that time it has built a solid reputation with music fans for its approach to scheduling the top indie acts from Japan and overseas.

5 Unit
MAP C2 ■ 1-34-17 Ebisu-Nishi, Shibuya-ku ■ 5459-8630 ■ See website for schedule ■ Adm ■ www.unit-tokyo.com
The top established club within walking distance of either Ebisu or Daikanyama. A basement venue with unusually high ceilings, it puts on a wide range of gigs and DJ sets, and plays hosts to everyone from Japanese indie-rock bands to international stars.

6 Womb
MAP A6 ■ 2-16 Maruyamacho, Shibuya-ku ■ 5459-0039 ■ Open 9pm–5am ■ Adm ■ www.womb.co.jp
Devotees of techno, house, and drum'n'bass will love this club, which has one of the largest dance floors in the city. A huge mirror ball hangs over the dance area, adding to an already impressive lighting system. Air-jet blasters keep things cool on the dance floor, and the club sprawls over four levels, each with its own bar.

Dancers on the stage at Womb

A popular jazz band performs at Blue Note Tokyo

7 Blue Note Tokyo

MAP S5 ■ 6-3-16 Minami-Aoyama, Minato-ku ■ 5485-0088 ■ Call for timings of shows ■ Adm ■ www.bluenote.co.jp

Cognoscenti claim this Tokyo branch – Japan's most famous jazz club – is just as good as sister venues in Paris or New York. Some of the world's hottest acts play here; the sets cover jazz, fusion, world music, and soul.

8 WWW

MAP Q5 ■ 13-17 Udagawacho, Shibuya-ku ■ 5458-7685 ■ See website for schedule ■ Adm ■ www-shibuya.jp

Live gigs take place all through the week with a wide range of local and international pop and rock artists. This central Shibuya venue was formerly a cinema.

9 Salsa Sudada

MAP T4 ■ Fusion Bldg 3F, 7-13-8 Roppongi, Minato-ku ■ 6447-1249 ■ Open 6pm–2am ■ Adm Fri, Sat

Salsa dancing has long been a fixture on the Tokyo club scene. Salsa Sudada is one of several Latin clubs in the city, attracting a crowd of local patrons, as well as Brazilian, Colombian, and Peruvian expatriates. Dance lessons are held every night at this extremely popular place.

10 AgeHa

MAP H6 ■ 2-2-10 Shin-Kiba, Koto-ku ■ 5534-2525 ■ Open Fri, Sat, occasional weekday events ■ Adm ■ www.ageha.com

Tokyo's largest nightclub has a huge main dancefloor and hosts famous DJs and live music. The outdoor spaces include a tented dance floor, a beach-themed seating area, and a bar-side swimming pool. It's at the end of the Yurakucho subway line, but the club runs buses to and from Shibuya Station all night.

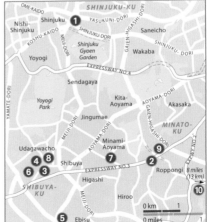

🔟 Restaurants

Low tables with *tatami* mats, Asakusa Imahan

1 Asakusa Imahan

This early exponent of beef dishes opened its first restaurant (see p91) in 1895. The specialty is *shabu-shabu*, wafer-thin slices of prime beef cooked at your table in a pot of boiling water and served with seasonal vegetables. Seating is at low tables on *tatami* mats.

2 Bird Land

The fame of this grill (see p85) rests on its high-quality *yakitori*, sticks of charcoal-broiled chicken doused in a slightly sweet soy-based sauce. Diners who are fond of *yakitori* will enjoy the chicken cuts here, which are closer to the lighter Chinese kebabs than the Turkish or Central Asian varieties. The restaurant offers a good wine list.

The sophisticated interior of Bird Land

3 Yoshiba

MAP H3 ▪ 2-14-5 Yokoami, Sumida-ku ▪ 3623-4480 ▪ Open 11:30am–2pm, 5–10pm Mon–Sat ▪ ¥¥

Wrestlers from the nearby sumo stables come here for *chankonabe* – a robust stew of vegetables, chicken, and fish. It's the staple diet of sumo wrestlers and the main dish served.

4 Kanda Yabu Soba

MAP F3 ▪ 2-10 Kanda-Awajicho, Chiyoda-ku ▪ 3251-0287 ▪ Open 11:30am–8pm ▪ ¥¥

In an old wooden building, this venerable restaurant serves classic Edo-period, handmade *soba* (buckwheat noodles) along with vegetable and pickle side dishes.

5 Hantei

MAP F1 ▪ 2-12-15 Nezu, Bunkyo-ku ▪ 3828-1440 ▪ Closed Mon ▪ ¥¥

Hantei specializes in delectable *kushiage*, deep-fried skewers of meat, fish, and vegetables served with small side dishes. Items are served six at a time, and the menu is set.

6 Maru

MAP M5 ▪ 6-12-15 Ginza, Chuo-ku ▪ 5537-7420 ▪ Open 11:30am–2pm, 5:30–11pm Mon–Sat ▪ ¥¥¥

This sleek restaurant, on the second floor, has a long counter table facing onto an open kitchen. It's a stylish place to sample the *kaiseki* style of fine dining at an affordable price.

7 Sushi Ouchi

MAP A6 ■ 2-8-4 Shibuya, Shibuya-ku ■ 3407-3543 ■ Open 11:40am–1:40pm, 5:30–10pm ■ ¥¥

At this sushi haven, the chef uses only natural ingredients and eschews MSG, chemical additives, and coloring. Even the soy sauce, vinegar, miso soup, and green tea that go with yellowtail, tuna, or conger eel are organic.

8 Higashi-Yama

MAP C2 ■ 1-21-25 Higashiyama, Meguro-ku ■ 5720-1300 ■ Open 11:30am–3pm Tue–Sat, 6pm–2am Mon–Sat ■ ¥¥¥

For a contemporary take on Japanese fine dining, it's worth searching out this sophisticated restaurant in the southwest of Tokyo. Opt for one of the tasting-course menus with exquisite dishes served on beautiful plates and bowls.

9 Sasanoyuki

MAP G1 ■ 2-15-10 Negishi, Taito-ku ■ 3873-1145 ■ Closed Mon ■ ¥¥

Many Tokyoites consider Sasanoyuki to be the city's finest tofu restaurant.

It has an illustrious history, with connections to the imperial family and the high priest at Kanei-ji temple during the Edo period, when the restaurant opened. The atmosphere is relaxed and the service unfussy.

10 Maisen

The popular Maisen chain (see p105) is famous for its delicious *tonkatsu* (deep-fried pork cutlets with their own brand of dipping sauce), served with rice, a bed of shredded cabbage, and miso soup. Seafood alternatives include delicately fried shrimp and oysters served with a dribble of lemon. The Shibuya-ku Maisen, located in an old converted bathhouse, is perhaps the most atmospheric branch to dine in.

Customers dining at the busy Maisen branch in Shibuya-ku

For a key to restaurant price ranges see p79

TOP 10 Cafés and Bars

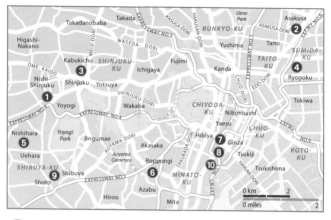

1 New York Bar
MAP T3 ■ 3-7-1-2 Nishi-Shinjuku, Shinjuku-ku ■ 5323-3458 ■ Open 5pm–midnight Sun–Wed (to 1am Thu–Sat)

You don't need to be staying at the Park Hyatt to enjoy its sophisticated bar, which featured prominently in the movie *Lost in Translation*. There's a cover charge after 8pm (7pm Sunday), and live music nightly featuring jazz from top artists.

New York Bar in the Park Hyatt hotel

2 Kamiya Bar
MAP R3 ■ 1-1-1 Asakusa, Taito-ku ■ 3841-5400 ■ Open 11:30am–10pm Wed–Mon

The oldest Western-style bar in town, this Tokyo institution was established in 1880. The bar was set up by Kamiya Denbei, who also built Japan's first brandy distillery. Once favored by writers and artists, the bar still serves its signature *denki-bran*, a cocktail made with cognac, gin, and wine.

3 Golden Gai
This bustling quarter (*see p107*), filled with scores of tiny bars housed in two-story wooden buildings, has hung on in Shinjuku since just after World War II. Most bars have a theme and only some are welcoming to tourists, but it's still well worth a visit.

4 Popeye
MAP G3 ■ 2-18-7 Ryogoku, Sumida-ku ■ 3633-2120 ■ Open 5–11:30pm Mon–Sat

Conveniently located within walking distance from the famous Sumo Stadium, this convivial bar does its best to cater to Tokyo's unquench-able thirst with some 70 beers on tap, including the city's best selection of Japanese beers.

5 Sasagin
MAP A5 ■ 1-32-15 Uehara, Shibuya-ku ■ 5454-3715 ■ Open 5–11:45pm Mon–Sat

This is a great place to sample different types of Japanese sake.

Tastes range from the syrupy sweet to the highly rated acerbically dry. Top-grade sake, such as the divine *dai-ginjo*, is served chilled.

6 Pink Cow
MAP U4 ■ Roi Bldg B1F, 5-5-1 Roppongi, Minato-ku ■ 6434-5773 ■ Open 5pm–8am daily ■ www.thepinkcow.com

Popular with the ex-pat crowd, this American-owned, lively bar and gallery space serves up good cocktails. It is not a bad place for dinner either, with reasonably priced international fare.

7 Cha Ginza
MAP M4 ■ 5-5-6 Ginza, Chuo-ku ■ 3571-1211 ■ Open 11am–6pm Tue–Sun

A shortened version of the Japanese tea ceremony here includes whisking the creamy brew into a bubbly froth and serving it with a Japanese sweet. The second floor serves *sancha* (ordinary green leaf tea).

8 Café de l'Ambre
MAP M5 ■ 8-10-15 Ginza, Chuo-ku ■ 3571-1551 ■ Open noon–10pm Mon–Sat (to 7pm Sun)

One of Tokyo's longest-running coffee shops, this place has been in business since 1948. Make your choice from the 30-odd blends including quite a few aged varieties. The retro ambience of the place is priceless and makes for an unforgettable visit.

Rows of beer taps at Goodbeer Faucets

9 Goodbeer Faucets
MAP A6 ■ Crossroad Bldg 2F, 1-29-1 Shoto, Shibuya-ku ■ 3770-5544 ■ Open 4pm–midnight (to 3pm Sat & Sun) ■ www.goodbeerfaucets.jp

The craft beer scene in Japan has blossomed in recent years. This centrally located spot is a superb place offering more than 40 craft beers on tap in a stylish, sophisticated setting. The food here is also a cut above the usual pub fare.

10 TwentyEight
MAP M6 ■ Conrad Tokyo, 1-9-1 Higashi-Shinbashi, Minato-ku ■ 6388-8745 ■ Open 8am–midnight

Located on the 28th floor of the Conrad Tokyo hotel, this stylish bar offers stellar cocktails, superb snacks, and gentle jazz piano music. With its subdued lighting and floor-to-ceiling windows, TwentyEight offers spectacular views over Tokyo Bay and is one of the most romantic spots in town.

Great views from TwentyEight

☰10 Markets, Stores, and Shopping Streets

Grand Mitsukoshi in Nihonbashi

① Mitsukoshi
MAP P2 ■ 1-4-1 Nihonbashi Muromachi, Chuo-ku ■ 3241-3311

This is the head branch of Japan's oldest department store business, founded in 1673. Aside from the many items on sale, it's worth visiting for its grand interior decorations, including a giant statue of the Goddess of Sincerity dominating the first floor. Get there early to see the hundreds of uniformed staff who bow respectfully to customers as they open the store each day.

② Toyosu Fish Market
MAP H6 ■ 6-chome Toyosu, Koto-ku ■ www.shijou.metro.tokyo.jp/index.html

Tokyo Metropolitan Central Wholesale Produce Market, better known as Tsukiji Fish Market, moved to these sparkling, state-of-the-art premises, across Tokyo Bay in Toyosu. This is the location of the famous tuna auctions that take place early in the morning.

③ Tsukiji Outer Market
The fish market (see p82) may have moved but there are still hundreds of vendors in the Tsukiji Outer Market, which has styled itself as the premier place to go food shopping in central Tokyo. There's plenty to see and taste here among the intricate streets, so pick up a map from the Information Center (Plat Tsukiji).

④ Naka-dori
MAP F4 ■ 1-chome to 3-chome Marunouchi, Chiyoda-ku

This tree-lined, flagstoned street is Maranouchi's main commercial spine, along which you'll find many international and local fashion boutiques as well as contemporary sculptures. The trees are illuminated with thousands of LED bulbs every winter.

⑤ Takeshita-dori
It's great for people watching and trend-spotting, but avoid this narrow Harajuku shopping street (see p102) if you're not keen on crowds. The stores here have their fingers firmly on the pulse of teen fashions, hence it's usually busy.

⑥ Venus Fort
MAP D2 ■ Palette Town, 1-3-15 Aomi, Koto-ku ■ 3599-0700 ■ Open 11am–9pm (11pm for some restaurants)

A cross between a mall and a theme park, Venus Fort was built to re-create the atmosphere of an 18th-century northern Italian city, with a changing, artificial twilight sky. The main focus among its many boutiques and stores is on cutting-edge brands in fashion, jewelry, and cosmetics.

Shoppers at Venus Fort

7 Ameyoko Market
MAP F2 ▪ Ueno Station

From modest beginnings as a postwar black market specializing in sweets made from potato, Ameyoko has developed into an amazing street with over 500 stalls and small stores built under the JR railway tracks. A favorite spot for very fresh food goods, especially fish.

8 Yanaka Ginza
This shopping street *(see p32)* may be quite small, but it's lined with some 70 independent businesses. Yanaka Ginza is characterized by the Edo period and offers a rare slice of traditional shopping. Look out for sculptures of cats on the buildings, a nod to the many strays that pad around the area.

Wickerwork for sale, Yanaka Ginza

9 mAAch ecute
MAP F3 ▪ 1-25-4 Kanda-Sudacho, Chiyoda-ku ▪ Open 11am–9pm Mon–Sat (to 8pm Sun) ▪ www.maach-ecute.jp

The decommissioned Manseibashi Station and the arches under the train tracks have been transformed into this stylish shopping and dining complex. Browse chic home goods and artisan foods from across Japan.

10 Coredo Muromachi
MAP P2 ▪ 2-2-1 Nihonbashi-Muromachi, Chuo-ku ▪ 3242-0010 ▪ Open 10am–9pm ▪ www.31urban.jp/lng/eng/muromachi.html

This stylish retail complex is split over three buildings. Zone in on Coredo Muromachi 3 for contemporary Japanese home and fashion design as well as gourmet foods.

TOP 10 ARTS STORES

Itoya, a stationery emporium

1 Itoya
MAP C3 ▪ 2-7-15 Ginza, Chuo-ku, ▪ 3561-8311
Nine floors with all kinds of stationery.

2 Bingo-ya
MAP C1 ▪ 10–6 Wakamatsu-cho, Shinjuku-ku ▪ 3202-8778
A selection of local folk arts and crafts.

3 Tokyu Hands
MAP R5 ▪ 12-18 Udagawa-cho, Shibuya-ku ▪ 5489-5111
DIY, crafts, hardware, and home items.

4 Takumi
MAP M5 ▪ 8-4-2 Ginza, Chuo-ku ▪ 3571-2017
Folk crafts, ceramics, and traditional toys.

5 Japan Traditional Crafts Aoyama Square
MAP C5 ▪ 8-1-22 Akasaka, Minato-ku ▪ 5785-1301
Traditional Japanese crafts.

6 Blue & White
MAP J6 ▪ 2-9-2 Azabu-Juban, Minato-ku ▪ 3451-0537
Items in indigo-dyed blue and white.

7 Hara Shobo
MAP E3 ▪ 2–3 Kanda-Jinbocho, Chiyoda-ku ▪ 5212-7801
Woodblock prints and illustrated books.

8 Sagemonoya
MAP C3 ▪ Palais Eternal Bldg, 704, 4-28-20 Yotsuya, Shinjuku-ku ▪ 3352-6286
Sells hanging purses and pipe cases as well as carved wood sculptures.

9 Oriental Bazaar
MAP S4 ▪ 5-9-13 Jingumae, Shibuya-ku ▪ 3400-3933
Gifts and souvenirs on Omotesando.

10 2k540 Aki-Oka Artisan
MAP C3 ▪ 5-9 Ueno, Taito-ku ▪ 6806-0254
A lively market selling traditional and contemporary crafts.

Tokyo for Free

1 Shrines and Temples

Religious sites in Tokyo rarely charge admission and the city has literally thousands of free temples and shrines. Most architecturally interesting are Senso-ji temple *(see pp14–15)* and Meiji Shrine *(pp30–31)*.

Contrasting architecture in Tokyo

2 Architecture

Few cities are as adventurous in their architectural style as Tokyo, making it a pleasure to admire buildings old and new. Contrast the grand dames, such as Tokyo Station *(see p41)*, with more modern constructions, such as the Prada Aoyama Building *(see p49)*.

3 Public Art

Roppongi Hills *(see p94)* and Tokyo Midtown *(see p95)* are scattered with interesting pieces of

Relaxing in Yoyogi Park

sculpture and public art. In Shinjuku *(see pp106–9)*, check out the artworks surrounding Shinjuku I-Land, including pieces by Roy Lichtenstein.

4 Museums

Museum of Yebisu Beer: MAP C2; 4-20-1 Ebisu, Shibuya-ku; 5423-7255; 11am–7pm Tue–Sun; www. sapporoholdings.jp/english/guide/ yebisu ■ Meguro Parasitological Museum: MAP C2; 4-1-1 Shimo-Meguro, Meguro-ku; 3716-1264; 10am–5pm Wed–Sun; www. kiseichu.org

The entry is free for the Museum of Yebisu Beer – which tells the story of the famous Japanese beer – or the quirky Meguro Parasitological Museum – where you'll find jars filled with such stomach-churning exhibits as the world's longest tapeworm.

5 Viewing Observatories

For a great city view, the free 45th-floor observation deck at the Tokyo Metropolitan Government Building *(see p48)* is hard to beat. The glittering vistas from the upper floors of the Shibuya Hikarie *(see p103)* are equally seductive.

6 Yoyogi Park

The chief location for the 1964 Summer Olympics, Yoyogi Park *(see p51)* has become one of Tokyo's most

beloved open spaces. It's very lively on Sundays, when bands perform and rockabilly dancers mingle with a rainbow array of fashion tribes around the entrance near Meiji Shrine.

7 Origami Kaikan
MAP F2 ■ 1-7-14 Yushima, Bunkyo-ku ■ 3811-4025 ■ Open 9:30am–6pm Mon–Sat ■ www. origamikaikan.co.jp

Learn about the gentle art of paper folding at Origami Kaikan, a building that includes free exhibitions as well as a workshop, where you can watch artisans creating paper art.

Aerial view of Shibuya Crossing

8 Shibuya Crossing
The statue and mural of Hachiko, Tokyo's most famous canine, gets lost amid the crowds flowing around Shibuya Station. The crossing (also known as Shibuya Scramble) here (see p103), enveloped by giant LCD screens and neon lights, is one of Tokyo's most iconic sights.

9 Walking Tours
The city offers 10 different free guided tours starting from the Tokyo Metropolitan Government Building (see p109). Itineraries include a tea ceremony and a trip out to a nature park in the suburbs. For details visit www.gotokyo.org/en/guide-services/.

10 Ginza's Galleries
Ginza is all about high-end, fashionable shopping, but it costs nothing to enjoy the free shows at the area's many commercial art galleries.

TOP 10 Festivals and Events

Festivities on New Year's Day

1 New Year's Day
Jan 1–4

Millions of Japanese welcome the New Year with visits to Shinto shrines and Buddhist temples throughout Tokyo. The most popular venues are Meiji Shrine *(see pp30–31)* and Senso-ji temple *(see pp14–15)*, where bells are rung to celebrate the New Year.

2 Coming-of-Age Day
MAP B5 ▪ 1-1 Kamizonocho, Yoyogi, Shibuya-ku ▪ 3379-5511 ▪ 2nd Mon in Jan

The age of consent in Japan is 20, which is a milestone celebrated in Tokyo by ceremonies at major shrines. Meiji Shrine *(see pp30–31)*, where an archery display is held to mark the event, is one of the most popular venues.

3 Water Purification Rites
MAP F3 ▪ Kanda Myojin Shrine ▪ Jan 10–12

Cleansing rituals are held at several shrines throughout Tokyo in winter. Young men and women whose 20th birthdays fall in the same year stand in pools full of blocks of ice and douse themselves with freezing buckets of water.

4 Tokyo Marathon
MAP A4 ▪ Feb

The Japanese take pride in their marathon runners, particularly women, who have won gold medals in past Olympics. Competing is a serious business, with very strict entrance rules and requirements. The run begins at the Tokyo Metropolitan Government Building.

5 Horseback Archery
MAP S2 ▪ Sumida Park, Taito-ku ▪ Mid-Apr

Yabusame, or horseback archery, was integral to the samurai arts of war. During this event, men in samurai gear charge their mounts through Sumida Park, aiming to strike three targets in rapid succession.

6 Design Festa
May/Nov

This biannual event, Asia's largest art festival, features 7,000 Japanese as well as international artists, musicians, and performers from every conceivable genre. Drawing over 50,000 visitors, this festival also presents fashion shows and *cosplay* exhibitionists. The 2-day event is held at Tokyo Big Sight *(see p56)*.

Design Festa display

7 Sanja Festival
MAP R2 ▪ Senso-ji Temple, 2-3-1 Asakusa, Taito-ku ▪ 3842-0181 ▪ 3rd weekend of May

Tokyo's largest festival honors two brothers who found a statue of Kannon, the Goddess of Mercy, in their fishing nets *(see p15)*. The spirits of the brothers and the shrine's deities are carried in portable shrines through the streets.

8 Kanda Matsuri

MAP F3 ▪ Kanda Myojin Shrine, 2-16-2 Soto-Kanda, Chiyoda-ku ▪ 3254-0753 ▪ Mid-May

One of Tokyo's three major festivals, the Kanda Matsuri is held in odd-numbered years. It features music and dance, but the highlight is the Heian-period costume parade, a procession of floats and *mikoshi* (portable shrines).

Kanda Matsuri parade

9 Sumida River Fireworks

Last Sat in July

Around 1 million Tokyoites converge on the riverbanks near Asakusa to see over 20,000 fireworks light up the skies and the Sumida River. The best views are from Komagata Bridge or between Shirahige and Kototoi bridges *(see pp16–17)*.

10 Seven-Five-Three Festival

Nov 15

Children who have reached the ages of three, five, or seven are dressed up in pint-sized traditional kimonos and taken to shrines to pray for their well-being at this delightful event. The numbers signify ages once considered milestones when child mortality was high. The occasion is also a great photo opportunity.

Children dressed for Seven-Five-Three Festival

TOP 10 FLOWER AND PLANT EVENTS

Plum flowers in full bloom

1 Plum Blossom Viewing
MAP F2 ▪ Late Jan–early Mar
The blossoms at Yushima Tenjin Shrine attract Tokyoites.

2 Cherry Blossom Viewing
Early–mid-Apr
Crowds picnic under the pink blossoms in parks and gardens.

3 Azalea Festival
MAP E1, L2 & M2 ▪ Apr 10–May 15 ▪ Adm
Azaleas bloom at Nezu Shrine and the Imperial Palace East Gardens.

4 Peony Displays
MAP F2 ▪ Mid-Apr
Pink, red, and yellow peonies can be viewed at Ueno Park's Tosho-gu shrine.

5 Iris Viewing
MAP B5 & D1 ▪ Early–mid-Jun
Visit the stunning iris gardens at Meiji Shrine and Horikiri.

6 Morning Glory Fair
MAP C1 ▪ Jul 6–8
Vendors sell potted morning glories in the grounds of Kishimojin Temple.

7 Chinese Lantern Plant Fair
MAP R1 ▪ 3842-0181 ▪ Jul 9–10
Popular fair held in Senso-ji temple.

8 Lotus Blossoms
MAP F2 ▪ Mid-Jul–Aug
An array of pink lotuses bloom in Shinobazu Pond in Ueno Park.

9 Chrysanthemum Festival
MAP B4 & C4 ▪ Late Oct–mid-Nov
Shinjuku Gyoen garden has an exhibition of chrysanthemums.

10 Fall Leaves
Late Nov
Red maples, russet fall leaves, and yellow ginkgoes bloom in the parks and old Edo-period gardens.

Tokyo
Area by Area

The Shinjuku skyline, emblazoned with neon signs

📻 Central Tokyo

The historic city and the site of Edo Castle, with its moats, stone ramparts, and bridges, once defined the imperial power structure: the merchant classes to the east, and samurai and lords to the south and west. In some ways, the power structure has remained visibly intact, with the Imperial Palace (on the site of the former Edo Castle) at the center; National Diet (parliament), law courts, and police headquarters to the south; and the financial center to the east. The area has been transformed by a series of fires, earthquakes, air raids, and developers, yet the outlines of the core city remain intact. Modern-day central Tokyo has also developed as a lively tourist attraction with excellent sightseeing and shopping options around every corner.

Light on the decorative Nihonbashi Bridge

CENTRAL TOKYO

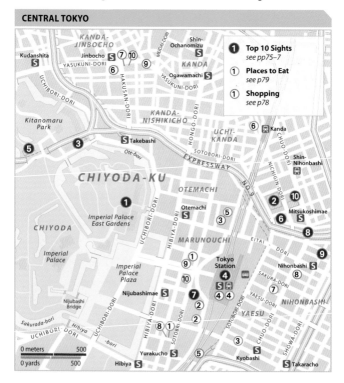

① **Top 10 Sights**
see pp75–7

① **Places to Eat**
see p79

① **Shopping**
see p78

Imperial Palace East Gardens, with a view of the tea pavilion

1 Imperial Palace East Gardens

MAP L2 ■ 1-1 Chiyoda, Chiyoda-ku ■ Open Mar–14 Apr: 9am–4:30pm Tue–Thu, Sat & Sun (15 Apr–Aug: to 5pm; Sep–Oct: to 4:30pm, Nov–Feb: to 4pm)

The gardens were designed by Kobori Enshu in the 17th century and opened to the public in 1968. The nucleus of this design can be seen in the pond area, with its waterfall, stone lantern, bridge, tea pavilion, and pebbled beach. The garden is resplendent with plum blossoms, spring cherry, and azaleas in spring; irises and lilies in summer; and bush clover, camellias, and maple leaves in the fall.

2 Bank of Japan

MAP N2 ■ 2-1-1 Nihonbashi-Hongokucho, Chuo-ku ■ 3279-1111 ■ English-language tour: 2:45–3:45pm Tue

The bank was aptly built on the site of the shogun's former gold mint. Kingo Tatsuno, who designed Tokyo Station, was responsible for this earlier 1896 building. The Bank of Japan is divided into two sections – the New Building where financial transactions occur and the Old Building which has a few offices, is more of an architectural exhibit. The building represents the first Western-style building designed by a Japanese architect.

3 National Museum of Modern Art (MOMAT)

MAP L1 ■ 3-1 Kitanomaru-koen, Chiyoda-ku ■ 5777-8600 ■ Open 10am–5pm Tue–Thu, Sat & Sun (to 8pm Fri) ■ Adm ■ www.momat. go.jp/english

Visitors can take a look at the exhibitions that draw on this museum's excellent collection of over 9,000 works from leading Japanese artists, past and present, plus some important European pieces. The range of art on display here is impressive, including gilded screens, woodblock prints, and striking video works.

Painting by Édouard Manet at MOMAT

The elegant red-brick Tokyo Station

4 Tokyo Station
MAP N3 ▪ 1-chome Marunouchi, Chiyoda-ku

Designed by Kingo Tatsuno, this 1914 red-brick building recently underwent a major restoration that brought back its twin cupolas. Rendered in Queen Anne style, it is said to be modeled on Station Amsterdam Centraal. The south side of the building is occupied by a hotel and the north by the small but interesting Tokyo Station Gallery, hosting regularly changing exhibitions.

> **BUILDING EDO CASTLE**
>
> When completed in 1640, Edo Castle was the largest citadel in the world, with 30 bridges, 28 armories, 21 watch-towers, and 110 gates. Gigantic slabs of stone were shipped from Izu Peninsula to make impregnable walls. More than 100 men were hired to drag the stones from the ship. The stones have survived; the wooden castle has not.

5 Crafts Gallery
MAP K1 ▪ 1-1 Kitanomaru-koen, Chiyoda-ku ▪ 5777-8600 ▪ Open 10am–5pm Tue–Sun ▪ Adm

Beautifully finished in brick and stonework, the 1910 building housing this museum once served as the headquarters of the Imperial Guard. Today, it showcases *mingei*, folk craft products representing a mid-20th-century movement that saw beauty through the use and aging of objects. There are fine examples of pottery, textiles, ceramics, lacquer, glass, metal, and bamboo ware. Exhibitions tend to focus on single themes, with individual artists using traditional methods and materials.

6 Currency Museum
MAP N2 ▪ 1-3-1 Nihonbashi-Hongokucho, Chuo-ku ▪ 3277-3037 ▪ Open 9:30am–4:30pm Tue–Sun

Operated by the Bank of Japan, this museum has a dizzying variety of currencies from the past and present on display, along with money-related items from around the world. There are also some hands-on exhibits.

7 Intermediatheque
MAP M3 ▪ 2-7-2 Marunouchi, Chiyoda-ku ▪ 5777-8600 ▪ Open 11am–6pm Tue–Thu & Sun (to 8pm Fri & Sat) ▪ Adm ▪ www.intermediatheque.jp/en

This is one of Tokyo's most eclectic and interesting museums, displaying key pieces from the collection of the University of Tokyo – from dinosaur skeletons to contemporary art.

8 Nihonbashi Bridge
MAP P2 ▪ Nihonbashi, Chuo-ku

Occupying a special place in Tokyo's history, Nihonbashi is shown in many *ukiyo-e* woodblock prints. The current structure dates from 1911. In the run-up to the 1964 Tokyo Olympics, waterways were filled in and a system of overhead expressways built. Distances throughout Japan are still measured from the bronze pole here, called the Zero Kilometer marker.

Nihonbashi Bridge

Exhibits adorned with beautiful artwork at the Kite Museum

⑨ Kite Museum
MAP P3 ▪ Taimeiken 5F, 1-12-10 Nihonbashi, Chuo-ku ▪ 3275-2704 ▪ Open 11am–5pm Mon–Sat ▪ Adm ▪ www.taimeiken.co.jp/museum.html

Displaying around 3,000 kites from all over the world, the museum focuses on Japan and China. The Japanese kites are adorned with real and mythological figures, as well as animals and natural landscapes, such as waves and sacred mountains. Kite frames are made from bamboo, and the sails from *washi*, a strong paper made from a type of mulberry tree. Picture outlines are painted in black India ink to restrict the flow of pigments.

⑩ Mitsui Memorial Museum
MAP P2 ▪ 2-1-1 Nihonbashi-Muromachi, Chuo-ku ▪ 5777-8600 ▪ Open 10am–5pm Tue–Sun ▪ Adm ▪ www.mitsui-museum.jp

Treasures of Japanese and Asian art collected down the generations by the Mitsui family are displayed in this elegant museum, housed in the grand, early 20th-century Mitsui Main Building. Among the delightful items displayed is a reconstruction of the interior of the celebrated Joan tea-ceremony room in Inuyama.

A DAY EXPLORING HISTORICAL SITES

Yasukuni Shrine — *Kudanshita Station* — *Kudan Kaikan Hotel* — *Budokan* — *Kitanomaru Park* — *Crafts Gallery* — *Imperial Palace East Gardens* — *Mandarin Oriental Tokyo* — *Site of Edo Castle* — *Babasaki Moat* — *Tokyo Station*

▶ MORNING

Arrive at Kudanshita Station around 10am after the commuter crowds have dispersed. Exit the station on Yasukuni-dori avenue and take a sharp left, where the 1930s Kudan Kaikan Hotel stands, a blend of nativist and Art Deco styles. Return to the main road and walk uphill to **Yasukuni Shrine** *(see p42)*, a fine piece of Shinto architecture. Forego the military museum in favor of strolling the pleasant grounds, full of cherry trees. Have lunch beside the garden pond.

AFTERNOON

Return to the main road, cross, and follow the signpost to Tayasu-mon, a wooden gate leading into **Kitanomaru Park** *(see p12)*. Before seeing the gate, note an old Meiji-era tower. Past the gate, linger outside the octagonal **Budokan** *(see p12)*, the martial arts hall where the Beatles once played concerts. Follow the road south and visit the **Crafts Gallery**, housed in the former headquarters of the Imperial Guard. Afterwards, stroll around the pretty **Imperial Palace East Gardens** *(see p75)*, the site of Edo Castle, the shogun's citadel. Here, you can climb the ruins of a keep for a view of the gardens. Press on south toward Babasaki Moat, home to white swans, egrets, and turtles. Cross busy Hibiya-dori and walk toward the nearby **Tokyo Station**, a superb 1914 structure. Have a drink at the Mandarin Bar in the sumptuous **Mandarin Oriental Tokyo** hotel *(see p128)*.

See map on p74 ←

Shopping

1 Shin-Marunouchi Building

MAP M3 ■ 1-5-1 Marunouchi, Chiyoda-ku ■ 5218-5100

The expansive shopping mall housed in this skyscraper boasts more than 150 stores and eateries, ranging from boutiques and jewelers to bakeries.

Interior of the Kitte shopping mall

2 Kitte

MAP M3 ■ 2-7-2 Marunouchi, Chiyoda-ku ■ 3216-2811

The former Central Post Office building was transformed into a shopping mall. It offers an excellent selection of local retailers special-izing in fashion, household goods, and traditional crafts with a contemporary flair.

3 Oazo

MAP N2 ■ 1-6-4 Marunouchi, Chiyoda-ku ■ 5218-5100

This dazzling glass complex of stores, restaurants, and cafés also has a massive English bookstore, Maruzen.

4 Tokyo Character Street

MAP N3 ■ B1 First Avenue Tokyo Station, 1-9-1 Marunouchi, Chiyoda-ku ■ 3210-0077

Lovers of Japanese pop culture should zone in on this collection of stores devoted to beloved comic book and TV characters, including Hello Kitty and Ultraman.

5 Muji

MAP M4 ■ 3-8-3 Marunouchi, Chiyoda-ku ■ 5208-8241

This is the world's largest store for the globally acclaimed "no-brand brand" that sells quality clothing, furnishings, and housewares.

6 Hara Shobo

MAP E3 ■ 2-3 Kanda-Jinbocho, Chiyoda-ku ■ 5212-7801

This specialist offers a huge variety of woodblock prints. These range from affordable prints that cost around ¥10,000 to pieces that are worthy of being exhibited at museums.

7 Ebisu-do Gallery

MAP E3 ■ Inagaki Bldg 4F, 1-9 Kanda-Jinbocho, Chiyoda-ku ■ 3219-7651

This gallery specializes in *ukiyo-e* woodblock prints. Originals start at ¥25,000, but you can pick up a good reproduction for only around ¥3,000.

8 Yamamoto Yama

MAP P3 ■ 2-10-2 Nihonbashi, Chuo-ku ■ 3281-0010

In addition to serving fine Japanese teas and confections, tea-ceremony instruments, such as bamboo whisks, iron water pots, and ceramic tea bowls, can be purchased here.

9 Ohya Shobo

MAP E3 ■ 1-1 Kanda-Jinbocho, Chiyoda-ku ■ 3291-0062

Established in 1882, this store sells *ukiyo-e* woodblock prints and antique books at reasonable prices.

10 Isseido

MAP E3 ■ 1-7 Kanda-Jinbocho, Chiyoda-ku ■ 3292-0071

Dating from 1913, this antiquarian bookstore retains its original Art Deco features. The second floor has old English books and rare maps.

Places to Eat

PRICE CATEGORIES

Price ranges are for an average-size dinner for one. Lunchtime menus are usually less expensive.

¥ under ¥2,000   ¥¥ ¥2,000–¥10,000
¥¥¥ over ¥10,000

1 Brasserie aux Amis
MAP M3 ▪ Shin-Tokyo Bldg, 1F, 3-3-1 Marunouchi, Chiyoda-ku ▪ 6212-1566 ▪ ¥¥

Dine on rustic brasserie food in a charming setting and wash down your *plat du jour poisson* with a drink from the long wine list.

2 Bar de España Muy
MAP M3 ▪ Tokyo Bldg Tokia, 2F, 2-7-3 Marunouchi, Chiyoda-ku ▪ 5224-6161 ▪ ¥¥

Relax at this fun tapas bar serving Catalan-style food. Try the black squid with a glass of cava.

3 Dhaba India
MAP N3 ▪ Sagami Bldg, 1F, 2-7-9 Yaesu, Chuo-ku ▪ 3272-7160 ▪ ¥

This Southern Indian eatery offers thali sets and masala dosas served with basmati rice.

Masala dosa at Dhaba India

4 Tokyo Ramen Street
MAP N3 ▪ B1 First Avenue Tokyo Station, 1-9-1 Marunouchi, Chiyoda-ku ▪ ¥

Ramen restaurants run stalls with variations on the popular noodle dish.

5 Washoku En
MAP N2 ▪ Oazo Bldg, 5F, 1-6-4 Marunouchi, Chiyoda-ku ▪ 5223-9896 ▪ ¥¥

Feast on a fine selection of regional Japanese cuisine and simple dishes, such as grilled salmon belly and smoky eggplant.

6 Aroyna Tabeta
MAP M3 ▪ 3-8-7 Uchikanda, Chiyoda-ku ▪ 3526-2079 ▪ ¥

This modest eatery specializes in spicy, authentic Thai green and red curries and fried noodles.

7 Yukari
MAP N3 ▪ 3-2-14 Nihonbashi, Chuo-ku ▪ 3271-3436 ▪ Closed Sun ▪ ¥¥

Known for its delicately prepared fish dishes with mouthwatering relishes and seasoning. Try the conger eel, snapper, and crab with Japanese citrus.

8 Roast Chicken House
MAP M3 ▪ New Tokyo Bldg, B1, 3-3-1 Marunouchi, Chiyoda-ku ▪ 5220-5588 ▪ Closed Sun & public holidays ▪ ¥¥

As the name suggests, the specialty at this restaurant is succulent, free-range Date chicken. Wines, sake, and juices are organic.

9 Salt
MAP M3 ▪ Shin-Marunouchi Bldg, 6F, 1-5-1 Marunouchi, Chiyoda-ku ▪ 5288-7828 ▪ ¥¥

Crisp Australian wines are perfect complements for the fusion fish dishes that are served here.

10 Breeze of Tokyo
MAP M3 ▪ Marunouchi Bldg, 36F, 2-4-1 Marunouchi, Chiyoda-ku ▪ 5220-5551 ▪ ¥¥

Superb French cuisine is presented in a very chic setting with great views over the city. There is an extensive list of cocktails and wines and 30 different types of champagne.

See map on p74

🔟 Ginza

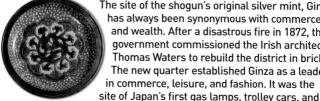

The site of the shogun's original silver mint, Ginza has always been synonymous with commerce and wealth. After a disastrous fire in 1872, the government commissioned the Irish architect Thomas Waters to rebuild the district in brick. The new quarter established Ginza as a leader in commerce, leisure, and fashion. It was the site of Japan's first gas lamps, trolley cars, and Western-style department stores. The epicenter of Ginza is the 4-chome district, a crossing dominated by modern stores. Though a premier cosmopolitan shopping and cultural experience, with its teahouses, incense and calligraphy stores, high-end sushi restaurants, and the very traditional Kabukiza theatre, it is also firmly Japanese.

Plate at the Idemitsu Museum of Arts

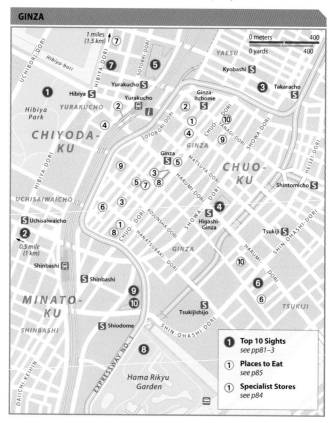

GINZA

① Top 10 Sights
see pp81–3

① Places to Eat
see p85

① Specialist Stores
see p84

1 Hibiya Park
MAP L4 ■ 1 Hibiya Koen, Chiyoda-ku ■ 3501-6428

Built over a former military parade ground converted from the estates of shogun Ieyasu's less-favored Outer Lords, Hibiya Park was rebuilt as Japan's first Western-style park in 1903. European features, such as bandstands, a rose garden, an open-air theater, and a bronze heron fountain overlooked by a wisteria trellis, are set against a small but exquisite Japanese garden, with rock placements and cherry trees lining paths at the center of the park.

2 Japan Sake and Shochu Information Center
MAP M4 ■ 1-16-15 Nishi-Shinbashi, Minato-ku ■ 3573-2371 ■ Open 10am–6pm Mon–Fri ■ www.japan sake.or.jp/sake/english/goto/jssic.html

For those interested in knowing more about Japan's national beverage of sake and *shochu*, the center has a museum where visitors can sample 50 different types of sake, *shochu* and *awamori* (distilled rice liquor).

3 National Film Archive of Japan (NFAJ)
MAP N4 ■ 3-7-6 Kyobashi, Chuo-ku ■ 5777-8600 ■ Call for timings ■ Adm ■ www.momat.go.jp

The only center in Japan devoted to the study and dissemination of

Inside National Film Archive of Japan

Japanese and foreign films, the NFAJ holds almost 40,000 films in its collection, including many restored Japanese classics. Besides its two theaters, there is a library of books on film and a gallery featuring exhibitions of stills, photographs, and film-related items. The NFAJ sometimes runs programs of Japanese cinematic masterpieces, usually with English subtitles.

4 Kabukiza Theatre
MAP N5 ■ 4-12-15 Ginza, Chuo-ku ■ 3545-6800 ■ www.kabuki-bito.jp/eng

One of Ginza's most striking buildings is this theater devoted to the performing art of Kabuki. Rebuilt in recent years so that a soaring tower block could be added (in which is located a small museum), the theater's frontage features giant purple banners, lanterns, and colorful posters.

Flamboyant facade of Kabukiza Theatre

Interior of Tokyo International Forum

5 Tokyo International Forum

MAP M3 & M4 ■ 3-5-1 Marunouchi, Chiyoda-ku ■ 5221-9000 ■ www. t-i-forum.co.jp/english

One of the city's architectural wonders, the majestic Tokyo International Forum was designed by Rafael Viñoly and completed in 1996. It functions as a premier culture convention center, with four graduated cubes encased in granite, abutting a high, tapering trajectory of glass and steel, aptly named Glass Hall. Crossing the skywalks among the glass and girders at the transparent apex of the building, above cantilevered areas and atria, is like walking across a crystal suspended above the city.

6 Tsukiji Outer Market

MAP F6 ■ Tsukiji, Chuo-ku

Even though the old fish market has departed for new premises in Toyosu, the old food businesses of the outer market remain and make for mouth-watering browsing. There are ample chances for grazing on street food, buying souvenirs, such as crockery, tea, and kitchen knives, and discovering Tsukiji Uogashi, the new center for food vendors.

7 Idemitsu Museum of Arts

MAP M3 ■ Teigeki Bldg, 9F, 3-1-1 Marunouchi, Chiyoda-ku ■ 5777-8600 ■ Open 10am–5pm Tue–Sun (to 7pm Fri) ■ Adm ■ www.idemitsu.co.jp/museum

As petroleum tycoon Sazo Idemitsu's fortune increased, so did his passion for collecting Japanese and Asian art. Opened in 1966, the museum bearing his name displays a diverse, eclectic collection of artworks, which includes paintings, bronzes, ceramic ware, *ukiyo-e* prints, lacquer, and rare gold-painted screens. Its calligraphy holdings include the world's largest collection of works by the Zen monk Sengai. Works from China, Korea, and the Middle East are also periodically displayed. The room containing pottery shards affords tremendous ninth-floor views of the Imperial Palace grounds.

8 Hama Rikyu Garden

MAP M6 ■ 1-1 Hama Rikyu Teien, Chuo-ku ■ 3541-0200 ■ Open 9am–5pm ■ Adm

The younger brother of shogun Ietsuna had parts of the bay filled in and a villa built here in 1654. Completed by a later shogun, Ienari, the basic design and balance of the garden remain gloriously intact. The highlight is a large tidal pond, with a small tea pavilion, and islets connected by wooden bridges. Over 600 species of peony, in addition to crepe myrtle, cherry, iris, bamboo, and plum, grow in the garden today.

Tranquil Hama Rikyu Garden

9 Shiodome and Caretta Shiodome

MAP M5 ■ 1-8-2 Higashi-Shinbashi, Minato-ku ■ 6218-2100

Resembling a futuristic mini-city, the bayside Shiodome features a grove of skyscrapers, notably Shiodome Media Tower and the highly regarded Conrad Tokyo hotel, as well as an Italian-style outdoor piazza, cafés, restaurants, and cocktail bars. The 47-story Caretta Shiodome houses more than 60 stores, restaurants, and cafés.

TAISHO CHIC

Popular culture thrived in Ginza during the Taisho period (1912–26), as a more liberal mood blew through the city. The age saw the appearance of the "Modern Girl," a product of European fashions, the American Jazz Age, and film divas. With their bobbed hair, these girls typified the confidence of a new age that challenged Japanese values.

10 Ad Museum Tokyo

MAP M5 ■ Caretta Shiodome, B1F–B2F, 1-8-2 Higashi-Shinbashi, Minato-ku ■ 6218-2500 ■ Open 11am–6pm Tue–Sat ■ www.admt.jp

Sponsored by advertising giant Dentsu in 2002, this spacious museum traces the history of Japanese advertising beginning from the Edo period to this day and age. It displays advertising publications and the exhibits run from colored woodblock prints to the latest TV commercials. The museum library has over 150,000 digitally saved advertisements.

A DAY SHOPPING IN GINZA

Map showing: Mikimoto Ginza 2, Kimuraya, Hattori Building, Christain Dior Building, Matsuya, Ginza Station, Mitsukoshi, Dover St Market Ginza, Uniqlo, Lion Beer Hall, Le Café Doutor Ginza

▶ MORNING

Leave Ginza Station at the 4-chome exit well before 10am and have coffee at the elegant Le Café Doutor Ginza. Walk across to the **Mitsukoshi** *(see p66)* department store opposite in time to be greeted by staff when it opens. Stroll a few steps to the svelte Christian Dior Building and then return to the 4-chome crossing. On the opposite corner, visit Wako, another department store. It is located in the **Hattori Building** *(p41)*, a symbol of Ginza since the early 1930s. Next door, the bakery **Kimuraya** *(see p84)* specializes in *anpan*, a local delicacy since 1875. Return to Mitsukoshi, with its trademark bronze lions, and browse its high-quality goods. Spare a few minutes to ascend to the roof, where offerings are left at a Shinto shrine to promote prosperity. Visit the food basement for a light lunch or green tea and Japanese sweets.

AFTERNOON

Cross the road and walk northeast along Chuo-dori, passing **Mikimoto Ginza 2** *(see p84)*, the originator of cultured pearls, and the department store Matsuya, which has a Design Gallery on its seventh floor showcasing items by Japan's top designers. Afterwards, visit some of the area's more recent retail entrants: the main Tokyo branch of fast-fashion retailer Uniqlo, which is connected to the boutique Dover St Market Ginza. Slake your thirst at the famous Lion Beer Hall nearby.

See map on p80 ←

Specialist Stores

The quirky Mikimoto Ginza 2 building

 Mikimoto Ginza 2
MAP N4 ▪ 2-4-12 Ginza, Chuo-ku ▪ 3535-4611 ▪ www.mikimoto.com
Housed in an eye-catching building designed by Toyo Ito, Mikimoto Ginza 2 sells the type of exquisite cultured pearls first developed by Kokichi Mikimoto in 1893.

2 Akomeya
MAP M4 ▪ 2-2-6 Ginza, Chuo-ku ▪ 6758-0271 ▪ www.akomeya.jp
Many varieties of rice as well as items made from the grain, such as sake, feature at this classy grocery and homewares store and café.

3 Akebono
MAP M4 ▪ 5-7-19 Ginza, Chuo-ku ▪ 3571-3640
The store specializes in *wagashi*, Japanese confections eaten with green tea, which are made from traditional ingredients such as *anko* (sweet red bean paste). Branches can be found in Tokyo's department stores.

4 Sayegusa
MAP M5 ▪ 4-4-4 Ginza, Chuo-ku ▪ 3573-2441
A top-quality children's wear store that has been in business since 1869. Four floors of clothing, dresses, suits, and accessories.

5 Kimuraya
MAP M4 ▪ 4-5-7 Ginza, Chuo-ku ▪ 3561-0091
Set up in the 1870s, Kimuraya sells *anpan*, bread rolls that are stuffed with red bean paste.

6 Takumi
MAP M5 ▪ 8-4-2 Ginza, Chuo-ku ▪ 3571-2017
An interesting mix of folk crafts, ceramics, and traditional toys in a tasteful setting.

7 Ginza Natsuno
MAP M5 ▪ 6-7-4 Ginza, Chuo-ku ▪ 3569-0952
A small store with a huge selection of chopsticks. Light and portable, they make ideal souvenirs.

8 Kyukyodo
MAP M4 ▪ 5-7-4 Ginza, Chuo-ku ▪ 3571-4429
A venerable Japanese paper specialist, Kyukyodo has been in the trade since the 17th century. Gift cards, paper boxes, and incense are also on sale.

9 Niwaka
MAP N4 ▪ 2-8-18 Ginza, Chuo-ku ▪ 3564-0707
Original, custom-designed jewelry created by artisans in Kyoto workshops are a speciality here. The store also has a made-to-order service.

10 Tanagokoro
MAP N4 ▪ 1-8-15 Ginza, Chuo-ku ▪ 3538-6555
Purveyors of *binchotan*, a high-quality charcoal. Placed in a room or bath water, it is said to have curative powers and can also act as a purifier, humidifier, and deodorizer.

Places to Eat

1 Kyubei
MAP M5 ■ 8-7-6 Ginza, Chuo-ku ■ 3571-6523 ■ www.kyubey.jp/en ■ Closed Sun ■ ¥¥¥

The high temple of sushi, Kyubei offers an extraordinary eating experience, even if it breaks the bank.

2 Shin Hinomoto
MAP M4 ■ 2-4-4 Yurakucho, Chiyoda-ku ■ 3214-8021 ■ Closed Sun & public holidays ■ ¥¥

Owned and run by a Brit, this authentic *izakaya* (Japanese pub) prides itself on excellent fish.

3 Kanetanaka-an
7-6-16, Ginza, Chuo-ku ■ 3289-8822 ■ Closed Sun ■ ¥¥¥

Sample a refined *kaiseki* five-course banquet showcasing different aspects of Japanese cooking.

4 Robata
MAP M4 ■ 1-3-8 Yurakucho, Chiyoda-ku ■ 3591-1905 ■ ¥¥

Quality Japanese fare, including grilled food, tofu dishes, and salads, is served in an atmospheric setting.

5 Ten-Ichi
MAP M4 ■ 6-6-5 Ginza, Chuo-ku ■ 3571-1949 ■ www.tenichi.co.jp ■ ¥¥¥

This celebrity-endorsed tempura restaurant serves light, delicately fried fish and vegetable morsels direct from the pan.

Sophisticated interior at Ten-Ichi

PRICE CATEGORIES

Price ranges apply for an average-size dinner for one. Lunchtime menus are usually less expensive.

¥ under ¥2,000   ¥¥ ¥2,000–¥10,000
¥¥¥ over ¥10,000

6 Tsukiji Sushi-sei
MAP N5 ■ 4-13-9 Tsukiji, Chuo-ku ■ 3541-7720 ■ Closed Wed ■ ¥¥

Follow the crowd and ask for the reliable *omakase* (chef's choice) at this traditional, Edo-style sushi chain.

7 Bird Land
MAP M4 ■ Tsukamoto Sozan Bldg, B14, 4-2-15 Ginza, Chuo-ku ■ 5250-1081 ■ Closed Sun & Mon ■ ¥¥

Very popular for its fine-quality and fresh *yakitori* (grilled sticks of chicken seasoned with soy sauce), Bird Land also offers other succulent well-presented chicken dishes too.

8 Little Okinawa
MAP M5 ■ 8-7-10 Ginza, Chuo-ku ■ 3572-2930 ■ ¥¥

This restaurant brings the cuisine of Japan's southernmost islands to Tokyo. Try the Okinawa-style pork and noodle dishes.

9 Sato Yosuke
MAP M4 ■ Deihonkan, 1F, 6-4-17 Ginza, Chuo-ku ■ 6215-6211 ■ ¥

Serves traditional handmade *inaniwa udon*, noodles that originate from the snowy mountains of Akita Prefecture, with different side dishes.

10 Edogin
MAP N5 ■ 4-5-1 Tsukiji, Chuo-ku ■ 3543-4401 ■ ¥¥

With fish served straight from tanks, the savory sushi here could not be fresher. Servings are plentiful in a no-frills setting.

See map on p80 ◀

TOP10 Ueno, Asakusa, and Oshiage

Even in the 21st century, parts of northeastern Tokyo retain their old Edo *shitamachi* character. Ueno is home to museums, temples, and a cherry tree-filled park as well as a major train station. Dotted with religious sites, traditional restaurants and a wide range of shops, Asakusa appeals as much to the hedonist as to the Buddhist acolyte. Across the Sumida River, Oshiage has a retro appeal despite the looming presence of the contemporary Tokyo Skytree.

Tokyo National Museum

Ueno Park in fall

1 Ueno Park

This wonderful park *(see pp20–21)* is an engaging mix of leisure and culture. Among the highlights are the Tokyo National Museum, contemporary Japanese and Western art galleries, a science museum, avenues of cherry trees, and the Toshogu shrine – a fine historical monument. For visitors more interested in leisure activities, there are also restaurants, cafés, a zoo, and a huge pond divided into a boating area, conservation corner, and a magnificent lotus pond.

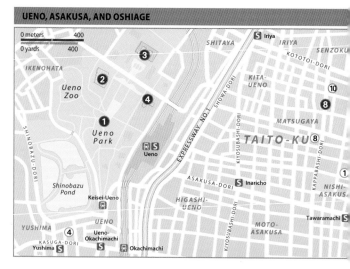

UENO, ASAKUSA, AND OSHIAGE

2 Tokyo Metropolitan Art Museum

MAP F1 ■ 8-36 Ueno Koen, Taito-ku
■ 3823-6921 ■ Open 9:30am–5:30pm
Tue–Sun except 1st & 3rd Mon of the
month ■ Adm ■ www.tobikan.jp

Designed by architect Kunio Maekawa,
this red-brick building has partially
underground floors that may not be
the perfect place to present art, but
the exhibits are always interesting.
The main hall shows an eclectic
mix, ranging from Japanese flower
arrangements and ink-brush works
to contemporary installations.

Museum of Nature and Science

3 Tokyo National Museum

This acclaimed museum *(see
pp24–7)* is the centerpiece of Ueno
Park. Its exhibits are divided between
four main galleries: the Honkan
displays a collection of Japanese arts
and archeology; the Toyokan features
arts and crafts from Asia, with an
emphasis on Chinese, Central Asian,
and Korean objects; the Heiseikan
houses ancient archeological objects,
including pottery and burial statues;
and the Gallery of Horyu-ji Treasures
is home to a permanent collection of
precious religious artifacts. Also within
the complex is the Hyokeikan, a fine
example of Meiji-era architecture.

4 National Museum of Nature and Science

MAP F1 ■ 7-20 Ueno Koen, Taito-ku
■ 3822-0111 ■ Open 9am–5pm
Tue–Sun ■ Adm

A giant whale model outside the
building announces this enormous
museum, which is divided into the
original, renovated section and a
newer annex. Older displays and
exhibits of dinosaurs, asteroids,
fossils, and a reconstructed house
made from mammoth tusks vie
with modern touch-screen panels,
video displays, and models.

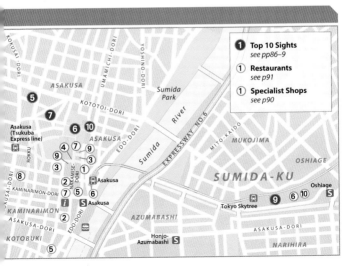

- **1** Top 10 Sights
  see pp86–9
- **1** Restaurants
  see p91
- **1** Specialist Shops
  see p90

Artisan at work, Edo-Shitamachi Traditional Crafts Museum

5 Edo-Shitamachi Traditional Crafts Museum

MAP R2 ■ 2-22-13 Asakusa, Taito-ku ■ 3842-1990 ■ Open 10am–8pm

Also known as Gallery Takumi, this museum was set up to preserve and promote local craft industries and techniques dating from the Edo period. Over 300 displays represent 50 different traditional crafts, with demonstrations on weekends.

6 Senso-ji Temple

Tokyo's mother temple *(see pp14–15)* looms majestically at the end of Nakamise-dori, an avenue of stores selling iconic trinkets. Two imposing gates lead to the great incense burner standing before the cavernous main hall, designed in a style known as *gongen-zukuri*. Within the same compound, Asakusa Shrine was founded in 1649 and rebuilt several times. Erected even earlier, the nearby 1618 Niten-mon gate remains completely intact, a miraculous survivor of earthquakes, typhoons, and air raids.

7 Hanayashiki

MAP R1 ■ 2-28-1 Asakusa, Taito-ku ■ 3842-8780 ■ Open 10am–6pm daily ■ Adm

Once part of an aristocratic residence to the west of Senso-ji temple, the Hanayashiki gardens were opened in the Asakusa Rokku entertainment district in 1853, with a small zoo added 20 years later. An Asakusa institution, this amusement park retains its retro quality, with old-fashioned game machines that complement an eerily realistic ghost house dating from the 1950s and Japan's oldest rollercoaster.

Ornate exterior of Senso-ji temple

⑧ Kappabashi Kitchenware Town

MAP Q2 ▪ Kappabashi-dori, Taito-ku

A long street, Kappabashi-dori is known by its sobriquet, "Kitchen Town." Two stores, Maizuru and Biken, are highly rated by connoisseurs of plastic food. Food samples have generated interest as a minor, collectable pop art. Viewed on an empty stomach, they can seem like works of towering genius.

⑨ Tokyo Skytree

MAP H2 ▪ 1-1-2 Oshiage, Sumida-ku ▪ 0570-55-0634 ▪ Open 8am–10pm ▪ www.tokyo-skytree.jp

Opened in 2012, the 2,080-ft (634-m) Tokyo Skytree has two observation decks. Although the architect sought to create a futuristic building, several traditional Japanese elements went into its design. Even the color is based on the traditional Japanese blueish-white color called *aijiro*.

Tokyo Skytree dominates the skyline

⑩ Amuse Museum

MAP R2 ▪ 2-34-3 Asakusa, Taito-ku ▪ 5806-1181 ▪ Open 10am–6pm Tue–Sun ▪ Adm ▪ www.amusemuseum.com

Multiple patched and mended garments are the main features of this diverting museum. The fabrics are like expressionist paintings in rustic colors. There's also a digital exhibition of classic *ukiyo-e* (woodblock prints) and a viewing terrace providing panoramas over neighboring Senso-ji temple and Tokyo Skytree.

See map on p86–7

A DAY IN OLD ASAKUSA

▶ MORNING

Exit Asakusa Station, walk north along Umamichi-dori to Kototoi-dori. Turn left and the **Edo-Shitamachi Traditional Crafts Museum** is a short walk away. The nearby **Hanayashiki** Amusement Park is a relic of the old entertainment district of Rokku. Southwest of Hanayashiki stretches the Rokku Broadway, a pedestrian street that still boasts a few traditional theaters as well as comedy and story-telling halls, including **Asakusa Engei Hall** *(see p59)*. Stop to look at the street performers, posters and lively barkers outside on Rokku Broadway. The narrow backstreets around Denboin-dori have many cheap, but characterful, restaurants serving fried noodles and *oden*, a fish-cake hot pot.

AFTERNOON

Walk south to the great **Kaminari-mon** *(see p14)*, the main entrance to **Senso-ji temple** *(see pp14–15)* to admire the giant paper lantern and the ancient guardian statues. Walk toward the **Sumida River** *(see pp16–17)* and the station where you began. Turn right on Edo-dori for Gallery ef, housed in an earth-walled, 19th-century storehouse, a rarity in contemporary Tokyo. The café here is excellent. Retrace your steps to the station and stop at the brightly painted Azumabashi Bridge, where traditional pleasure boats, *yakatabune*, are moored. Return to the corner of Kaminari-mon and Umamichi streets to visit the **Kamiya Bar** *(see p64)*, for *denki-bran*, its trademark drink.

Specialist Shops

Shoppers enjoy some retail therapy at Solamachi

1 Bengara
MAP R3 ▪ 1-35-6 Asakusa, Taito-ku ▪ 3841-6613 ▪ Open 10am–6pm daily (except 3rd Sun of the month) ▪ www.bengara.com
Sells over 300 designs of linen *noren* – traditional split curtains hung above doors of stores and homes.

2 Bunsendo
MAP R3 ▪ 1-30-1 Asakusa, Taito-ku ▪ 3844-9711 ▪ Open 10:30am–6pm
The specialty here are the folding fans used by Japanese dancers, Kabuki actors, and geisha.

3 Fujiya
MAP R2 ▪ 2-2-15 Asakusa, Taito-ku ▪ 3841-2283 ▪ Open 10am–6pm Fri–Wed
Tenugui (printed cotton towels) make great practical souvenirs, and this store has hundreds of designs.

4 Ojima
MAP R2 ▪ 2-3-2 Asakusa, Taito-ku ▪ 4285-9664 ▪ Open 9am–5pm ▪ www.edokiriko.jp
Ojima is the place to buy delicate sake cups and glasses, with engraved patterns on colored glass.

5 Kurodaya
MAP R3 ▪ 1-2-5 Asakusa, Taito-ku ▪ 3844-7511 ▪ Open 11am–7pm Tue–Sun
This store specializes in *washi* (Japanese paper), woodblock prints, and other paper novelties.

6 Solamachi
MAP H2 ▪ 1-1-2 Oshiage, Sumida-ku ▪ Open 10am–9pm ▪ www.tokyo-solamachi.jp
Sushi-shaped fridge magnets, incense, decorative fans, chopsticks, and anime character goods are all sold in this large mall beneath Tokyo Skytree.

7 Sukeroku
MAP R2 ▪ 2-3-1 Asakusa, Taito-ku ▪ 3844-0577 ▪ Open 10am–6pm
Established in 1866, this is the only store in the city that makes and sells miniature Edo-style dolls and toys.

8 Inujirushi
MAP R2 ▪ 2-18-1 Nishi-Asakusa, Taito-ku ▪ 5830-3542 ▪ Open 10am–8pm
This store sells fashionable canvas bags, which come in a variety of hard-wearing, waterproof styles.

9 Yonoya Kushiho
MAP R3 ▪ 1-37-10 Asakusa, Taito-ku ▪ 3844-1755 ▪ Open 10:30am–6pm Thu–Tue
The place to come for boxwood combs, hair, and *netsuke* ornaments since 1717. The combs can last for generations if properly cared for.

10 Soi
MAP Q2 ▪ 3-25-11 Nishi-Asakusa, Taito-ku ▪ 6802-7732 ▪ Open 11am–6pm Tue–Sun
One of Tokyo's best homeware shops, with a great selection of ceramics.

➤ *See map on p86–7*

Restaurants

PRICE CATEGORIES

Price ranges are for an average-size
dinner for one. Lunchtime menus are
usually less expensive.

¥ under ¥2,000   ¥¥ ¥2,000–¥10,000
¥¥¥ over ¥10,000

1 Sometaro
MAP Q3 ▪ 2-2-2 Nishi-Asakusa,
Taito-ku ▪ 3844-9502 ▪ ¥

The only dish served here is
okonomiyaki – pancakes made with
shrimp, octopus, and vegetables.

2 Namiki Yabu Soba
MAP R3 ▪ 2-11-9 Kaminarimon,
Taito-ku ▪ 3841-1340 ▪ Closed Thu ▪ ¥

This ever-popular *soba* (buckwheat
noodle) store is located just up the
road from Senso-ji temple.

3 Daikokuya
MAP R3 ▪ 1-38-10 Asakusa,
Taito-ku ▪ 3844-1111 ▪ ¥¥

Expect long lines for the delicious
fish and vegetable tempura dishes at
this popular eatery.

4 Ikenohata Yabu Soba
MAP H2 ▪ 3-44-7 Yushima,
Bunkyo-ku ▪ 3831-8977 ▪ Closed
Wed ▪ ¥

This branch of a popular *soba* chain
serves classic noodles in a thick broth
as well as the cold summer *soba*.

5 Komagata Dozeu
MAP R2 ▪ 1-7-12 Komagata,
Taito-ku ▪ 3842-4001 ▪ ¥¥

Grilled and stewed loach, a small fish
resembling an eel, has been served
in time-honored fashion at this
restaurant since it opened in 1801.

6 Otafuku
MAP Q2 ▪ 1-2-6 Hanakawado,
Taito-ku ▪ 3871-2521 ▪ Closed Mon
▪ ¥¥

This charming century-old restaurant
specializes in *oden*, items such as
scallops, fish cake, boiled egg, and
chunks of radish simmered in a broth.

7 Maguro Bito
MAP R3 ▪ 2-18-12
Kaminarimon, Taito-ku ▪ 3847-7139
▪ ¥

Expect great value for money from
this *kaitenzushi* (conveyor belt sushi)
restaurant, one of the most popular
in Tokyo, where the specialty is
maguro (tuna).

8 Asakusa Imahan
MAP Q2 ▪ 3-1-12 Nishi-
Asakusa, Taito-ku ▪ 3841-1114 ▪ ¥¥

Shabu-shabu consists of wafer-thin
cuts of beef dipped and cooked in a
boiling broth at your table and served
with vegetables and rice. This is one
of the best places to experience it.

Sleek decor at Asakusa Imahan

9 Waentei-Kikko
MAP R2 ▪ 2-2-13 Asakusa,
Taito-ku ▪ 5828-8833 ▪ Closed Wed
▪ ¥¥

Refined Japanese cuisine in an
informal setting. Diners can enjoy a
shamisen (Japanese banjo) recital.

10 Rokurinsha
MAP H2 ▪ 6th floor, Tokyo
Solamachi, 1-1-2 Oshiage, Sumida-ku
▪ 5809-7368 ▪ ¥

Join the line at this legendary ramen
stall, located beneath Tokyo Skytree,
to sample its chunky, chewy noodles
dipped in a separate bowl of
flavorsome broth.

Following pages Red torii (gates) at Hie Shrine

🔟 Roppongi and Akasaka

Roppongi is a major center for the arts, shopping, communications, and lifestyle, and it is Tokyo's premier nightlife district. Here, you will find innovative centers and facilities, including Roppongi Hills and Tokyo Midtown. Nearby Akasaka is filled with contemporary buildings, but political deals are still brokered in the rarefied air of chic restaurants and hotels. The area is also home to some revered temples and shrines.

Detail of the exterior of Nogi Shrine

① Roppongi Hills
MAP D6 ■ 6-10-1 Roppongi, Minato-ku ■ 6406-6000 ■ www.roppongihills.com

Opened in 2003, this sprawling city-within-a-city includes gardens and a live-performance area. The central structure, the 54-story Mori Tower, houses offices, more than 200 stores, restaurants, bars, the Grand Hyatt hotel, and the Mori Art Museum.

Roppongi Hills, a lively complex

ROPPONGI AND AKASAKA

❶	Top 10 Sights see pp94–7
①	Places to Eat see p99
①	Clubs and Bars see p98

2 Nogi Shrine
MAP C5 ■ 8-11-27 Akasaka, Minato-ku ■ 3478-3001

This modest but significant shrine honors General Maresuke Nogi, who, along with his wife, committed ritual suicide on September 13, 1912 in an act of loyalty when Emperor Meiji died. The event divided the country into those who admired the act as a heroic gesture, and those who condemned it as an archaic practice. The general's house stands beside the shrine and is open on the eve and anniversary of the couple's death.

3 Tokyo Midtown
MAP D5 ■ 9-7-1 Akasaka, Minato-ku ■ 3475-3100 ■ www.tokyo-midtown.com

Unveiled in 2007, the Tokyo Midtown development set aside 40 percent of the complex for the landscaped Hinokicho Park and Midtown Garden. Midtown Tower and its core of buildings contain offices, apartments, shops, restaurants, bars, and the Ritz-Carlton Tokyo hotel. The area's cultural credentials are enhanced by the fascinating Suntory Museum of Art and 21_21 Design Sight, a design gallery conceived by architect Tadao Ando and fashion guru Issey Miyake.

4 Hie Shrine
MAP J4 ■ 2-10-5 Nagatacho, Chiyoda-ku ■ 3581-2471 ■ www.hiejinja.net/en

Burned down in the air raids of 1945 and rebuilt in 1958, Hie Shrine was originally erected as a protective shrine. Its role of deflecting evil spirits from Edo Castle is seen in wood carvings to the left of the main shrine, depicting a monkey protectively holding a baby. Pregnant women still come here to pray for safe deliveries, and the biannual festival Sanno Matsuri – a procession celebrating the imperial family – begins and ends at the shrine.

National Art Center's grand interior

5 National Art Center, Tokyo
MAP C6 ■ 7-22-2 Roppongi, Minato-ku ■ 5777-8600 ■ Open 10am–6pm Wed–Mon (to 8pm Fri) ■ Adm ■ www.nact.jp

Japan's largest exhibition space, the National Art Center, Tokyo hosts temporary exhibitions, such as Nitten, an annual event highlighting Japanese and Western painting, sculpture, craftwork, and calligraphy. Built in 2007, the space features an undulating glass facade, slated walls, and a wooden floor.

Atmospheric Hie Shrine

Statues of foxes stand guard at Toyokawa Inari Shrine

6 Toyokawa Inari Shrine and Temple

MAP D5 ■ 1-4-7 Moto-Akasaka, Minato-ku ■ 3408-3414

A Zen temple with Shinto elements, the shrine is distinctive for its orange banners, lanterns, and hundreds of statues of foxes representing the bodhisattva Jizo (protector of children and travelers), and Kannon, (the Goddess of Mercy). Behind the main buildings are forest-like paths lined with *senbon nobori* streamers hung by devotees in the hope of fulfilling their wishes. Eateries inside the shrine serve tasty *oden* (fish cake stew) and *kitsune soba* (buckwheat noodles).

7 Musée Tomo

MAP K5 ■ Nishi-Kubo Bldg, 4-1-35 Toranomon, Minato-ku ■ 5733-5131 ■ Open 11am–6pm Tue–Sun ■ Adm ■ www.musee-tomo.or.jp

Established in 2003 by Tomo Kikuchi, a collector of contemporary ceramics, this small museum is one of the most elegant in Tokyo. Exhibitions change every few months, highlighting a particular craftsperson or a school of ceramic ware, such as Bizen or Raku.

8 Tokyo Tower

MAP K6 ■ 4-2-8 Shiba-koen, Minato-ku ■ 3433-5111 ■ Open 9am–10pm

When opened in 1958 as a broadcasting mast, this Eiffel Tower clone was the tallest building in Tokyo. Despite its shabby aquarium, trick art museum, tacky waxworks, and souvenir stores, it attracts a number of visitors spurred by nostalgia and the fame of a 2005 film of the same name.

Tokyo Tower against the sky

ROPPONGI STREET ART

Many world-class artists were asked to create works on and around Roppongi Hills. Louise Bourgeois's huge spider sculpture, *Maman*, is the most visible, but there are also wall drawings, an illuminated robot, a giant coffee bean installation, digital screen models, a 3-D landscape painting, and waveform furniture such as benches.

9 Zojo-ji Temple
MAP E6 ■ 4-7-35 Shiba-koen, Minato-ku ■ 3432-1431 ■ Open 9am–5pm ■ www.zojoji.or.jp/en

Another victim of World War II air raids, Zojo-ji temple is a 1970s ferro-concrete reconstruction. The original temple was founded in 1393 and then removed to its present location, close to Tokyo Tower, in 1598. In the next century, it was chosen by the Tokugawa shoguns as their ancestral temple. Today, the temple hosts many religious events. The main hall contains ancient statues, written sutras, and other sacred objects, while the Ankokuden hall holds the Black Image of Amida Buddha, known as a miracle-working buddha that gives victory and defends against evil.

Ankokuden hall, Zojo-ji Temple

10 San-mon Gate
MAP E6 ■ Shiba-koen, Minato-ku

Fires and earthquakes have been reducing Tokyo's buildings to rubble for over 400 years, but the San-mon gate, the main entrance to Zojo-ji temple, has remained miraculously intact. The oldest wooden structure in the city, it was erected in 1605. The three tiers of the red-lacquered gate, an Important Cultural Treasure, represent the three stages required to enter Nirvana. The gate looks especially awesome at night, when it is illuminated.

A DAY IN THE ART TRIANGLE

▶ MORNING

Leave Roppongi Station by Exit 1, which leads directly into **Roppongi Hills** (see p94); at the top of the escalator is Louise Bourgeouis's *Maman*, a giant sculpture of a spider and one of many pieces of public art surrounding the shopping and business complex. Head to the top of Mori Tower for the excellent **Mori Art Museum** (see p45) and the urban vistas of the Tokyo City View observation deck. Cross Roppongi-dori and walk north to the **National Art Center, Tokyo** (see p95), a huge 12-room art venue where you can view an eclectic mix of art, displayed as part of a changing program of temporary exhibitions. You can also dine here at **Brasserie Paul Bocuse Le Musée** (see p99), set atop a massive inverted concrete cone. Take time to admire the views before setting off again.

AFTERNOON

Head north in the direction of **Nogi Shrine** (see p95), and then visit Gallery Ma. Sponsored by the bathroom appliance and fixtures company Toto, its exhibitions focus mainly on architecture and the latest trends in design. The gallery also has an excellent bookstore. Retrace your steps toward Roppongi Crossing to find **Tokyo Midtown** (see p95), where you can check out what's showing at either the Suntory Museum of Art or the **21_21 Design Sight** (see p51). **Bodega Santa Rita** (see p99), one of many restaurants and bars in the complex, is ideal for a drink and tapas after a day of sightseeing.

See map on p94 ←

Clubs and Bars

1 Alife
MAP T5 ▪ Econach Nishi-Azabu Bldg, 1-7-2, Nishi-Azabu, Minato-ku ▪ 5785-2531 ▪ Adm

Popular with locals and visitors alike, Alife serves up hip hop and R&B to visitors aged over 23.

2 Esprit Tokyo
MAP U5 ▪ Roppongi B & V Bldg, 2-3F, 5-1-6 Roponngi, Minato-ku ▪ 6230-0343

With state-of-the-art equipment and a high-tech disco ball, this favored club attracts famous DJs.

3 SuperDeluxe
MAP T5 ▪ 3-1-25 Nishi-Azabu, Minato-ku ▪ 5412-0515 ▪ www.super-deluxe.com

This bar, with an art and performance space, is where creative Tokyoites like to hang out. There are events most days.

4 Agave Clover
MAP T4 ▪ Clover Bldg B1F, 7-15-10 Roppongi, Minato-ku ▪ 3497-0229 ▪ Closed Sun

An expensive cantina-style drinking hole, with over 400 varieties of tequila.

5 Pink Cow
MAP U4 ▪ Roi Bldg B1F, 5-5-1 Roppongi, Minato-ku ▪ 6434-5773 ▪ www.thepinkcow.com

A favorite with expats, this lively bar and gallery is good for cocktails and California-Mexican food.

Quirky decor at Pink Cow

6 Muse
MAP C6 ▪ 4-1-1 Nishi-Azabu, Minato-ku ▪ 5467-1188 ▪ www.muse-web.com ▪ Closed Sun–Wed

A sought-after club, Muse is spread out over three levels, with lots of cozy chill-out areas.

7 Hobgoblin
MAP U4 ▪ Aoba Roppongi Bldg 1F, 3-16-33 Roppongi, Minato-ku ▪ 3568-1280 ▪ www.hobgoblin.jp

This English pub serves decent ale and British pub grub, such as bangers and mash and shepherd's pie.

8 Billboard Live
MAP T4 ▪ Tokyo Midtown Garden Terrace 4F, 9-7-4 Akasaka, Minato-ku ▪ 3405-1133 ▪ www.billboard-live.com

With two shows per day, this live music venue has a great line up. A glass wall provides superb city views.

9 Abbey Road
MAP U4 ▪ Roppongi Annex Bldg B1F, 4-11-5 Roppongi, Minato-ku ▪ 3402-0017 ▪ Adm

Top-quality tribute bands play on a revolving basis at this popular venue dedicated to the Beatles.

10 Propaganda
MAP U4 ▪ Yua Roppongi Bldg 2F, 3-14-9 Roppongi, Minato-ku ▪ 3423-0988 ▪ www.propaganda-tokyo.com

Popular and loud, this chic and well-stocked shot bar has English-speaking staff.

Places to Eat

PRICE CATEGORIES

Price ranges are for an average-size dinner for one. Lunchtime menus are usually less expensive.

¥ under ¥2,000   ¥¥ ¥2,000–¥10,000
¥¥¥ over ¥10,000

① RyuGin
MAP T4 ▪ Eisu Bldg, 7-17-24 Roppongi, Minato-ku ▪ 3423-8006 ▪ Closed Sun ▪ ¥¥¥

A remarkably innovative take on traditional *kaiseki* cuisine.

② Gonpachi
MAP C6 ▪ 1-13-11 Nishi-Azabu, Minato-ku ▪ 5771-0170 ▪ ¥¥

An enormous branch of the chain Japanese restaurant styled like an old Edo inn. The specialty is *kushiyaki*, charcoal-grilled skewers.

③ Fukuzushi
MAP U5 ▪ 5-7-8 Roppongi, Minato-ku ▪ 3402-4116 ▪ ¥¥

Beside the usual tuna and squid offerings are the less common shad, conger eel, and other delicacies at this no-frills sushi restaurant.

④ Inakaya East
MAP U4 ▪ 5-3-4 Roppongi, Minato-ku ▪ 3408-5040 ▪ ¥¥¥

An old-fashioned *robatayaki* (grilled food) eatery, offering all manner of meat and other foods.

⑤ Nodaiwa
MAP V5 ▪ 1-5-4 Higashi-Azabu, Minato-ku ▪ 3583-7852 ▪ Closed Sun ▪ ¥¥

Specializing in wild eel, Nodaiwa serves charcoal-grilled fish drizzled with an appetizing sauce.

⑥ Hassan
MAP T4 ▪ Denki Bldg B1, 6-1-20 Roppongi, Minato-ku ▪ 3403-8333 ▪ ¥¥

The star course here is the set, all-you-can-eat dinner of *shabu-shabu*, thin strips of high-quality beef dipped in boiling broth.

⑦ Chinese Café Eight
MAP T5 ▪ Court Annexe, 3-2-13 Nishi-Azabu, Minato-ku ▪ 5414-5708 ▪ ¥¥

A fun, informal 24-hour eatery that attracts a young crowd and serves excellent Chinese food. The specialties here are Peking Duck and dim sum.

⑧ Tofuya-Ukai
MAP W5 ▪ 4-4-13 Shiba-koen, Minato-ku ▪ 3436-1028 ▪ ¥¥¥

Gorgeous *kaiseki*-style meals, made up of tofu and seasonal ingredients, are served in this beautiful old wooden building set in a traditional garden at the foot of the Tokyo Tower.

Garden views at Tofuya-Ukai

⑨ Bodega Santa Rita
MAP T4 ▪ Tokyo Midtown Garden Terrace 1F, 9-7-4 Akasaka, Minato-ku ▪ 5413-3101 ▪ ¥¥

Seriously good wines and fine regional fare from southern Spain is served here. This place has charming stucco interiors.

⑩ Brasserie Paul Bocuse Le Musée
MAP T4 ▪ 3F National Arts Center, 7-22-2 Roppongi, Minato-ku ▪ 5770-8161 ▪ ¥¥

Located inside the striking National Arts Center building, this stylish restaurant serves light French cuisine. The fixed-price lunches are extremely popular.

See map on p94

TOP 10 Aoyama, Harajuku, and Shibuya

Omotesando-dori, the chic boulevard running through Aoyama and Omotesando, is Tokyo's fashion quarter. A shift in mood occurs as Omotesando segues into Harajuku and Takeshita-dori; the latter is a street humming with off-the-peg boutiques, street stalls, fast-food joints, and a young crowd. Giant video screens characterize Shibuya, which is lined with fashion and department stores, clubs, museums, art galleries, and cafés.

Stylish interior of the Nezu Museum

1 Nezu Museum

MAP C6 ▪ 6-5-1 Minami-Aoyama, Minato-ku ▪ 3400-2536 ▪ Open 10am– 5pm Tue–Sun ▪ Adm ▪ www.nezu-muse.or.jp

Behind sandstone walls, this museum was established by the Meiji-era tycoon and politician Kaichiro Nezu. Some of the collection's textiles, lacquerware, and ceramics are so rare they are registered as National Treasures. The most famous piece is Ogata Korin's screen painting *Irises*.

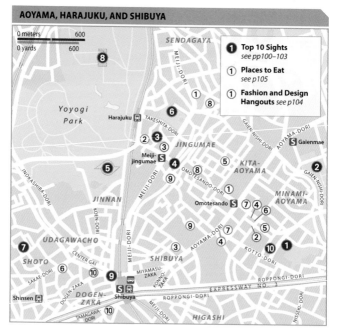

AOYAMA, HARAJUKU, AND SHIBUYA

1	**Top 10 Sights** see pp100–103
1	**Places to Eat** see p105
1	**Fashion and Design Hangouts** see p104

0 meters 600
0 yards 600

SENDAGAYA
Yoyogi Park
Harajuku
TAKESHITA-DORI
JINGUMAE
Meiji-jingumae
OMOTESANDO-DORI
KITA-AOYAMA
Gaienmae
MINAMI-AOYAMA
Omotesando
JINNAN
MEIJI-DORI
UDAGAWACHO
SHOTO
SHIBUYA
AOYAMA-DORI
KOTTO-DORI
ROPPONGI-DORI
Shinsen
DOGEN-ZAKA
Shibuya
ROPPONGI-DORI
EXPRESSWAY NO. 3
HIGASHI

Cherry blossoms as seen in spring, Aoyama Cemetery

② Aoyama Cemetery
MAP C5 ■ 2-32-2 Minami-Aoyama, Minato-ku

The graves of John Manjiro, the first Japanese person to go to America in the early 19th century, and Professor Ueno, the owner of the faithful dog Hachiko immortalized in bronze outside Shibuya Station, are here. Japan's first public cemetery explodes into clouds of pink petals each spring, when crowds of people visit for *hanami* (cherry blossom) viewing parties.

③ Ota Memorial Museum of Art
MAP B5 ■ 1-10-10 Jingumae, Shibuya-ku ■ 3403-0880 ■ Open 10:30am–5:30pm Tue–Sun ■ Adm ■ www.ukiyoe-ota-muse.jp

This remarkable museum has Tokyo's finest collection of *ukiyo-e* woodblock prints – about 14,000. The great names in this genre, such as Hiroshige, Utamaro, Hokusai, and Sharaku, all feature here. The collection was begun by Seizo Ota, a wealthy businessman who realized that many of the best works were being sold to foreign museums.

④ Omotesando
MAP R4

Even if you're not interested in shopping at the rows of designer boutiques here, strolling the length of tree-lined Omotesando is a pleasure, not least for its exceptional collection of contemporary buildings. There are buildings by nearly all of Japan's winners of the prestigious Pritzker Prize, including Tadao Ando (Omotesando Hills and Collezione), Kazuyo Sejima and Ryue Nishizawa of SANAA (Dior Building), and Toyo Ito (Tod's). It's also a great place for people-watching, particularly near Harajuku Station.

Taking a stroll down Omotesando

5 Yoyogi National Gymnasium

MAP Q4 ▪ 2-1-1 Jinnan, Shibuya-ku ▪ 3468-1171

A residential compound for American personnel during the Occupation (1945–52), the park area was called "Washington Heights." The Japanese government requested its return, turning the site into the Olympic Village in 1964 for the Tokyo Games. Architect Kenzo Tange designed the sweeping roofs of the pavilions at the southern end which still look modern.

Stylish Yoyogi National Gymnasium

6 Takeshita-dori and Togo Shrine

MAP B5 ▪ Harajuku, Minato-ku

On weekends, narrow Takeshita-dori is probably the single-most crowded spot in the entire city. The home of subculture kitsch, the lane is packed with theme clothing stores, takeout food, crêpe stands, and stores selling character items, cuddly toys, and all manner of quirky accessories. Just a few steps behind the street are the serenely quiet precincts of Togo Shrine. Dedicated to Admiral Heihachiro Togo, who engineered the defeat of the Russian fleet in 1905, the grounds offer a soothing escape from the heaving masses of Takeshita-dori.

7 Toguri Museum of Art

MAP A6 ▪ 1-11-3 Shoto, Shibuya-ku ▪ 3465-0070 ▪ Open 10am–5pm Tue–Sun (to 8pm Fri) ▪ Adm ▪ www.toguri-museum.or.jp

This small museum in a leafy residential area has an outstanding collection of Oriental porcelain. The Japanese collection includes fine examples of Imari and Nabeshima wares; the Chinese pieces represent the Tang, Song, and later dynasties. The highlight of the Korean section are fine Goryeo-era pieces.

8 Meiji Shrine

A massive gate, Ichi no Torii, marks the main entrance to the forested compound and outer grounds of Meiji Shrine (see pp30–31). Broadleaf trees and shrubs are planted beside gravel paths leading to the shrine. Burned to cinders in World War II, the current 1958 building is a faithful reproduction of the original shrine dedicated to Emperor Meiji, who died in 1912.

Visitors gather in front of the main Meiji Shrine building

Crowds at Shibuya Crossing

9 Shibuya Crossing
MAP Q6

Shibuya Station is undergoing a major redevelopment, which has resulted in the completion of the Shibuya Hikarie complex on the east side. But it's the crossing at the station's northwest corner that is the most famous sight here: the flow of people on the move surrounded by a blaze of neon and video screens is mesmerizing. Look for the statue and mural of the faithful dog Hachiko amid the crowds lingering in front of the station.

SHIBUYA STYLE

Shibuya is one of the major centers of street fashion in Tokyo and there have been many subculture trends that originated here. The iconic Shibuya 109 building, visible from Shibuya Crossing, offers some of the hottest brands as well as new and upcoming trends. A good place for noticing what young Japan likes to wear is Center Gai, a lively alley near Shibuya Crossing with popular stores, nightclubs, and fast food joints.

10 Taro Okamoto Memorial Museum
MAP C6 ■ 6-1-19 Minami-Aoyama, Minato-ku ■ 3406-0801 ■ Open 10am–6pm Wed–Mon ■ Adm ■ www.taro-okamoto.or.jp

The former studio of the famed Japanese artist Taro Okamoto (1911–1996), sometimes referred to as the Japanese Picasso, is now a museum. Founded in 1998 by his adopted daughter Toshiko, it re-creates the atmosphere of the artist's atelier.

A DAY OF ARCHITECTURE

▶ **MORNING**

After exiting Omotesando Station, stroll down Aoyama-dori until you see the open plaza outside the United Nations University on your right, designed by Kenzo Tange. Turn back the way you came until you glimpse **Spiral** *(see p46)* on the right. Return to the intersection at the subway and follow the road on the right up to the triangular outline of **Prada Aoyama** *(see p51)*. A little farther on, Collezione is the work of the self-taught architect, Tadao Ando. Kengo Kuma's design for the **Nezu Museum** *(see p100)* is at the southern end of **Omotesando** *(see p101)*. Return to the station area and head into the streets east of Omotesando to find the *tonkatsu* (pork cutlet) restaurant **Maisen** *(see p105)*.

AFTERNOON

The stretch of Omotesando heading towards Meiji-dori is lined with impressive architecture including the building for the leather goods store Tod's, designed by Toyo Ito, and **Omotesando Hills** *(see p104)*, a fashion brand complex with cool lines and angles. Take a left on Meiji-dori; a little farther on you can see the glass sections and counter-angles of the 2008 Audi Forum Tokyo, a building known as the Iceberg. Walk on to Shibuya Station, which is in the process of being redeveloped with new towers. One that has been completed is Shibuya Hikarie – its Sky Lobby on the 11th floor has great views and you can dine at d47 Shokudo in the complex.

See map on p100 ←

Fashion and Design Hangouts

1 Anniversaire Café
MAP S5 ▪ 3-5-30 Kita-Aoyama, Minato-ku ▪ 5411-5988
A terrace seat here doesn't come cheap, but this chic café is the place to see and be seen.

2 A Bathing Ape
MAP S5 ▪ 5-5-8 Minami-Aoyama, Minato-ku ▪ 3407-2145
One of Tokyo's most original fashion stores. The distinctive jeans and hoodies attract a very cool, discerning crowd.

3 Laforet Harajuku
MAP R4 ▪ 1-11-6 Jingumae, Shibuya-ku ▪ 3475-0411
The oddball styles offered by hundreds of clothes and accessory stores here attract teens. It's also a wonderful place to observe Tokyo youth and fashion fads.

4 Comme des Garçons
MAP S5 ▪ 5-2-1 Minami-Aoyama, Minato-ku ▪ 3406-3951
Curving glass windows and tilted walls hint at the creative approach to fashion here at Rei Kawakubo's main fashion store.

Showroom, Comme des Garçons

5 Undercover
MAP S5 ▪ Bleu Cinq Point Bldg, 5-3-22 Minami-Aoyama, Minato-ku ▪ 3407-1232
The brainchild of former punk musician Jun Takahashi, this store sells youth streetwear.

Prada Aoyama's amazing storefront

6 Prada Aoyama
MAP S5 ▪ 5-2-6 Minami-Aoyama, Minato-ku ▪ 6418-0400
Prada's quality, chic offerings are almost overshadowed by the brilliance of this crystal-like building.

7 Issey Miyake Men
MAP S5 ▪ 3-18-11 Minami-Aoyama, Minato-ku ▪ 3423-1407
The flagship store for men stylishly presents Miyake's highly original approach to fashion.

8 Omotesando Hills
MAP R4 ▪ 4- 12-10 Jingumae, Shibuya-ku ▪ 3497-0310
Boutiques, such as Jimmy Choo, and specialist stores, including e.m. jewelry, vie with other brands here.

9 Cat Street
MAP B5 ▪ Omotesando, Minato-ku
This quiet fashion road is home to an exciting assortment of edgy boutiques, stylish cafés, and hole-in-the-wall eateries.

10 Shibuya 109 Building
MAP B6 ▪ 2-29-1 Dogenzaka, Shibuya-ku ▪ 3477-5111
With a clientele rarely over 20, the cutting-edge clothes sold inside this cylindrical-shaped building are a measure of tomorrow's fashion trends.

Places to Eat

PRICE CATEGORIES

Price ranges are for an average-size dinner for one. Lunchtime menus are usually less expensive.

¥ under ¥2,000   ¥¥ ¥2,000–¥10,000
¥¥¥ over ¥10,000

1 Fonda de la Madrugada
MAP B5 ▪ Villa Bianca B1F, 2-33-12 Jingumae, Shibuya-ku ▪ 5410-6288 ▪ ¥¥

This authentic Mexican cantina offers enchiladas, stuffed chillies, and tortillas.

2 Jangara Ramen
MAP Q4 ▪ 1-13-21 Jingumae, Shibuya-ku ▪ 3404-5572 ▪ ¥

Tonkotsu ramen at Jangara Ramen

Tonkotsu (pork bone) ramen is the best of the Kyushu-style dishes that are on the menu here.

3 Beacon
MAP R5 ▪ 1-2-5 Shibuya, Shibuya-ku ▪ 6418-0077 ▪ ¥¥

An upmarket, self-styled urban chop house run by one of Tokyo's more innovative American chefs.

4 8ablish
MAP S5 ▪ 5-10-17 Minami-Aoyama, Minato-ku ▪ 6805-0597 ▪ ¥

This chic café offers a good range of vegetarian and vegan dishes, as well as organic beer and wine.

5 Maisen
MAP S4 ▪ 4-8-5 Jingumae, Shibuya-ku ▪ 3470-0071 ▪ ¥¥

Tonkatsu (deep-fried and breaded pork cutlets) are the specialty of this main branch of a well-known chain.

6 Gyossantei
MAP A6 ▪ Fontis Bldg, 2-23-12 Dogenzaka, Shibuya-ku ▪ 5489-6350 ▪ Closed Sun ▪ ¥¥

Offers the regional cuisine of Miyazaki Prefecture and other Kyushu dishes.

7 Ghungroo
MAP S5 ▪ Seinan Bldg, 5-9-6 Minami Aoyama, Minato-ku ▪ 3406-0464 ▪ ¥¥

Gungroo is a cut above many other Indian restaurants in Tokyo, a reputation gained for its delicious cuisine in elegant surroundings.

8 Mominoki House
MAP B5 ▪ 2-18-5 Jingumae, Shibuya-ku ▪ 3405-9144 ▪ ¥¥

This place mostly dishes up healthy portions of vegetarian fare, although there are some departures, such as the venison and fish dishes.

9 Las Chicas
MAP R5 ▪ 5-47-6 Jingumae, Shibuya-ku ▪ 3407-6865 ▪ ¥¥

Simple international and fusion cuisine, wines, and cocktails served by foreign waiters make Las Chicas a favorite with expats.

Diners at popular Las Chicas

10 Kanetanaka-so
MAP B6 ▪ Cerulean Tower Tokyu Hotel 2F, 26-1 Sakuragaoka, Shibuya-ku ▪ 3476-3420 ▪ ¥¥¥

A traditional, very urbane Japanese restaurant serving *kaiseki ryori*, Japan's seasonally changing and delicate haute cuisine.

See map on p100 ←

TOP10 Shinjuku

Resembling an all-purpose city, Shinjuku is replete with large parks, train stations, shopping complexes, and department stores. Railway lines split the area into two. The windy avenues in West Shinjuku are dominated by offices, stores, and experimental skyscrapers. East Shinjuku is a legacy of the 1960s, when the area's Bohemian quarter attracted artists, writers, and political activists. Though cultural features exist on both sides, East Shinjuku appears more hedonistic, with its neon-illuminated nightspots and a sprawling red-light district.

The neon lights of Kabukicho

1 Kabukicho
MAP B3 ▪ Kabukicho, Shinjuku-ku

Tokyo's premier *sakariba* (pleasure quarter), Kabukicho caters to the city's craving for indulgence. In the words of the American author Donald Richie, this garish, neon-lit district "concerns itself with the permissive indulgence that the old Edo kept alive on its stage." At night, its maze of clubs, cabarets, live-music houses, bars, and restaurants come to life.

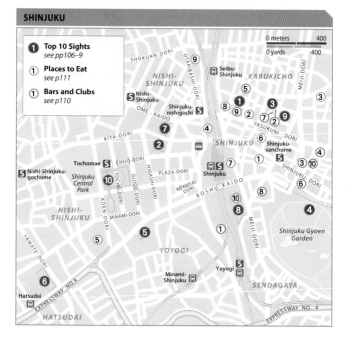

SHINJUKU

1	**Top 10 Sights**	see pp106–9
1	**Places to Eat**	see p111
1	**Bars and Clubs**	see p110

② Ricoh Imaging Square Shinjuku

MAP A3 ■ Shinjuku Center Bldg, 1F, 1-25-1 Nishi-Shinjuku, Shinjuku-ku ■ 3348-2941 ■ Open 10:30am– 6:30pm ■ Closed Tue & public holidays

Camera enthusiasts should not overlook this photo gallery, camera museum, and service center located in the Shinjuku Center Building. Besides the exhibitions of world-class photography and displays by gifted amateurs, there is a collection of almost every camera made by Pentax. The hands-on displays allow visitors to try out everything. The center's goal to "improve the photographic culture" includes events, lectures, and demonstrations of photo techniques that take place in their Open Studio.

③ Golden Gai

MAP B3 ■ Shinjuku, Shinjuku-ku

A labyrinth of over 200 tiny, time-warped watering holes clusters along Golden Gai's four pedestrian lanes. Dating from just after World War II, these bars are popular with local office workers, and are also patronized by writers, sumo wrestlers, and cross-dressers. Most of the establishments here charge a ¥1000 seating fee for starters.

④ Shinjuku Gyoen

MAP B4 ■ 11 Naito-machi, Shinjuku-ku ■ 3350-0151 ■ Open 9am–4:30pm Tue–Sun ■ Adm

Part of the estate of the Naito feudal clan, this large garden became an imperial retreat in 1906. Now open to the public, Shinjuku Gyoen offers Japanese, French, and English gardens, an old-fashioned greenhouse, and a traditional teahouse. Interestingly, tests have shown that the park is consistently two degrees or more cooler than the surrounding urban area.

Bunka Gakuen Costume Museum

⑤ Bunka Gakuen Costume Museum

MAP A4 ■ 3-22-7 Yoyogi, Shibuya-ku ■ 3299-2387 ■ Open 10am–4:30pm Mon–Sat ■ Adm

This remarkable museum is a part of Bunka Gakuen University, an elite fashion design school. It's historical collection, a fraction of which can be shown at a time, ranges from a Heian-era 12-layered elaborate kimono to costumes worn by Noh actors. More modern designs include the Japanese take on the Swinging Sixties. Scrolls and illustrations depict the types of clothing worn by Japanese people through the ages.

Shinjuku Gyoen

ETHNIC FOOD IN SHIN-OKUBO

The diversity of modern Tokyo can be best experienced in the cosmopolitan, but down-to-earth, Shin-Okubo district. It is home to almost every conceivable Asian nationality, hence its sobriquet, "Little Asia." Apart from Chinese eateries, Korean barbeques, and Burmese restaurants, the area also has several Thai, Indian, and Malaysian curry spots.

---

⑥ NTT InterCommunication Center

MAP A4 ■ Tokyo Opera City Tower, 4F, 3-20-2 Nishi-Shinjuku ■ 5353-0900 ■ Open 11am–6pm Tue–Sun ■ www.ntticc.or.jp

Part of the Tokyo Opera City office and culture complex, the center holds fascinating exhibitions that show the link between technology and creativity. Run by the telecom giant NTT, the permanent and temporary installations, video art, and interactive displays explore the connection between art, media design, and the latest techno wizardry. The excellent video library shows experimental films and video art, and features the work of cutting-edge artists, including Laurie Anderson and Nam June Paik.

Van Gogh's *Sunflowers*, Sompo Japan Nipponkoa Museum of Art

⑦ Sompo Japan Nipponkoa Museum of Art

MAP A3 ■ Sompo Japan Bldg, 42F, 1-26-1 Nishi-Shinjuku ■ 5777-8600 ■ Open 10am–6pm Tue–Sun ■ Adm ■ www.sjnk-museum.org/en

This museum was founded in 1976 to showcase the works of Seiji Togo (1897–1978), an artist whose images, mainly of women, hover between Art Deco, Cubism, and Japanese animation figures. There are also a number of paintings by European artists such as Gauguin and Cézanne. The insurance company that owns the building made news in the 1980s "bubble economy" years when it bought Van Gogh's *Sunflowers* for an unheard-of ¥5 billion.

⑧ Takashimaya Times Square

MAP B4 ■ 5-24-2 Sendagaya, Shinjuku-ku ■ 5361-1111 ■ Open 10am–8:30pm (department store – other shops may vary)

A shopping haven, this 15-story department store offers something for everyone. Besides the fashion and accessory departments, restaurants, cafés, and well-stocked food basement, there is a branch of Tokyu Hands, a large and fascinating hardware store packed with diverse items related to daily living. Of special interest to foreigners

NTT InterCommunication Center

is a branch of Kinokuniya, a huge bookstore with a floor set aside for books in English and other languages.

9 Hanazono Shrine
MAP B3 ▪ 5-17-3 Shinjuku, Shinjuku-ku ▪ 3209-5265

With orange pillars and vermillion walls, this shrine has been rebuilt several times since it was founded in the 16th century. Its presiding deity is Yamato Takeru, a legendary prince. Devotees stop by to petition the gods for luck. Rows of red and white paper lanterns illuminate the shrine's entrances at night.

The imposing Tokyo Metropolitan Government Building

10 Tokyo Metropolitan Government Building
MAP A4 ▪ 2-8-1 Nishi-Shinjuku, Shinjuku-ku ▪ 5321-1111 ▪ Open 9:30am–10:30pm

The Kenzo Tange-designed Tokyo Metropolitan Government Building (Tocho) is part of a grove of sky-scrapers that have been described as everything from a mini-Manhattan to a row of grave markers. The building's twin 48-story towers have observation rooms, and high-speed elevators carry visitors up in less than a minute. The 360-degree views from the top are superlative.

A DAY IN EAST SHINJUKU

▶ MORNING

Leaving the south exit of JR Shinjuku Station, walk down to **Shinjuku Gyoen** *(see p107)*, a spacious national garden. An entire morning can be spent here, but continue instead to **Takashimaya Times Square** *(see p108)*, a futuristic department store. Donatello's, on the 12th floor, serves good gelato, ice cream, and coffee. Take a short walk along Meiji-dori to the corner of Shinjuku-dori and Isetan, a department store and Tokyo institution. The fifth-floor Isetan Art Gallery showcases the latest trends in Japan's ceramic, print, and fine-art world. Walk up Shinjuka-dori, turn left and follow the road to **Tsunahachi** *(see p111)* on the right. The traditional restaurant serves tempura lunch sets at moderate prices.

AFTERNOON

Walk north until you reach the gates of **Hanazono Shrine**, whose grounds are right next to **Golden Gai** *(see p107)*, a quadrangle of bars; however, lanes will be fairly empty at this time. Walk into adjacent **Kabukicho** *(see p106)* and take almost any street north toward Okubo-dori, the main street cutting through Shin-Okubo. The district has many small temples and fox shrines, as well as Christian churches catering to a number of Korean worshipers. Have an early dinner at one of the several ethnic restaurants in Shin-Okubo before heading back to the bars of Golden Gai.

See map on p106 ←

Bars and Clubs

(1) Little Delirium
MAP V3 ■ Shinjuku Southern Terrace, 2-2-1 Yoyogi, Shibuya-ku ■ 6300-0807

This cozy Belgian bar offers an impressive range of bottled and draft beers, and good food.

(2) Albatross G
MAP V2 ■ 2F, 5th Avenue, 1-1-7 Kabukicho, Shinjuku-ku ■ 3203-3699 ■ Adm

The long counter, generous space, and ¥500 seating charge set this place apart from the usual run of cramped Golden Gai bars.

Jazz music at Shinjuku Pit Inn

(3) Shinjuku Pit Inn
MAP W3 ■ Accord Bldg, B1, 2-12-4 Shinjuku, Shinjuku-ku ■ 3354-2024 ■ Adm

Half-price weekend matinees are good value at this club, which is popular with serious jazz aficionados.

(4) Aiiro Café
MAP W3 ■ 7th Tenka Bldg, 1F, 2-18-1 Shinjuku, Shinjuku-ku ■ 6273-0740

Highly popular café bar that attracts a mixed, though mostly gay crowd.

(5) Shinjuku Loft
MAP V2 ■ Tatehana Bldg, B2F, 1-12-9 Kabukicho, Shinjuku-ku ■ 5272-0382 ■ Adm

At this long-established promoter of live rock and pop acts, the venue is divided into a main stage and a separate bar area.

(6) Open
MAP W3 ■ 2-5-15 Shinjuku, Shinjuku-ku ■ 3226-8855

This well-established nightspot is run by the people who set up one of Tokyo's first reggae bars back in the 1990s.

(7) Bar Plastic Model
MAP V2 ■ 1-1-10 Kabukicho, Shinjuku ■ 5273-8441

A 1980s music soundtrack throbs in the background at Bar Plastic Model, one of Golden Gai's more contemporary theme bars.

(8) Antiknock
MAP V3 ■ Rei Flat Bldg, B1F, 4-3-15 Shinjuku, Shinjuku-ku ■ 3350-5670 ■ Adm

Mainly dedicated to rock, this small club showcases up-and-coming acts, many of them appealing to Tokyo's chic cyber-punks.

(9) Garam
MAP V2 ■ Dai-Roku Polestar Bldg, 1-16-6 Kabukicho, Shinjuku-ku ■ 3205-8668

Practically a Tokyo institution, this small Kabukicho reggae bar is a welcoming and animated spot that features MCs and DJs as well as live acts. The music is a mix of dub, hip-hop, and roots reggae.

(10) Bar Gold Finger
MAP W3 ■ 2-12-11 Shinjuku, Shinjuku-ku ■ 6383-4649

A bar popular with the LGBTQ community in Shinjuku ni-chome, Tokyo's famous gay district. Dance events with DJs are a regular feature. Saturday nights are for women only.

Places to Eat

PRICE CATEGORIES
Price ranges are for an average-size dinner for one. Lunchtime menus are usually less expensive.

¥ under ¥2,000 ¥¥ ¥2,000–¥10,000
¥¥¥ over ¥10,000

View from New York Grill

 Tsunahachi
MAP V2 ■ 3-31-8 Shinjuku, Shinjuku-ku ■ 3352-1012 ■ ¥¥

Huge portions of deep-fried tempura served in a prewar building offer good value. English menu available.

2 Tokaien
MAP V2 ■ 1-6-3 Kabukicho, Shinjuku-ku ■ 3200-2934 ■ ¥¥

Over nine floors, Tokaien serves superb *yakiniku* (Korean-style barbecue). The sixth floor offers an all-you-can-eat menu.

 Sansar
MAP W2 ■ 6-13-8 Shinjuku, Shinjuku-ku ■ 3354-8553 ■ ¥¥

Friendly Nepali staff serve up a standard Indian repertoire, plus some delicious Nepalese specialties.

 Omoide-Yokocho
MAP V2 ■ Nishi-Shinjuku, 1-chome, Shinjuku-ku ■ ¥

This atmospheric warren of lanes is full of smoky *yakitori* chicken eateries, noodle stores, and bars.

An eatery in Omoide-Yokocho

 New York Grill
MAP T3 ■ Park Hyatt Hotel, 52F, 3-7-12 Nishi-Shinjuku, Shinjuku-ku ■ 5323-3458 ■ ¥¥¥

One of the leading grill restaurants in Tokyo, this eatery serves a great range of meat and seafood options.

6 Tavolo di Fiori
MAP V2 ■ 3-16-13 Shinjuku, Shinjuku-ku ■ 3354-3790 ■ ¥¥

A traditional trattoria, with authentic Tuscan fare served by genial staff.

7 Daidaiya
MAP V3 ■ Shinjuku Nowa Bldg 3F, 3-37-12 Shinjuku, Shinjuku-ku ■ 5362-7173 ■ ¥¥

Nouvelle Japanese and Asian fusion cuisine as well as more standard fare.

8 Ban Thai
MAP V2 ■ Dai-ichi Metro Bldg, 3F, 1-23-14 Kabukicho, Shinjuku-ku ■ 3207-0068 ■ ¥¥

This popular place was one of Tokyo's first authentic Thai restaurants.

9 Menya Musashi
MAP U3 ■ K1 Bldg, 1F, 7-2-6 Nishi-Shinjuku, Shinjuku-ku ■ 3363-4634 ■ ¥

It is widely regarded as among the best ramen eateries in Tokyo.

10 Imahan
MAP Q2 ■ Times Square Bldg, 14F, 5-24-2 Sendagaya, Shibuya-ku ■ 5361-1871 ■ ¥¥

Expect generous portions at this eatery known for *sukiyaki* (sliced meat with vegetables) and *shabu-shabu*.

See map on p106

🔟 Farther Afield

For more than 400 years, all roads have led to the city known today as Tokyo, the political, commercial, and cultural axis of Japan. Significant ports, trading posts, temples, mausoleums, and leisure resorts sprang up along these highways. As a result, ideas about architecture, religion, and gardening coursed into the city. A first-rate train service makes it easy to explore beyond the megalopolis, and for sights at the edges of the city, Tokyo's subway system is unmatched. Sumptuous tombs in Nikko, the ancient city of Kamakura, and the Edo-era Kawagoe invoke the past. Alternatively, hiking at Mount Fuji or Mount Takao is very rewarding, as is exploring Yokohama, Japan's second-largest city.

Naritasan Shinshoji temple

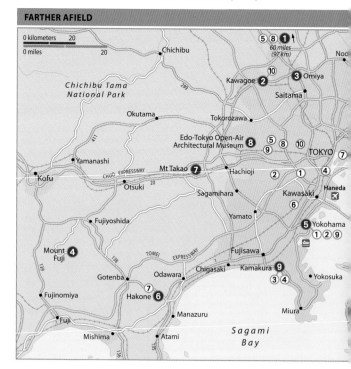

Detail of wood carvings at Toshogu shrine, Nikko

① Nikko

MAP B1 ▪ Nikko, Tochigi Prefecture ▪ Tobu Line from Asakusa ▪ Toshogu shrine Open 8am–5pm (to 4pm Nov–Mar) ▪ Adm

Nikko's opulent temples, religious art, sacred storehouses, and tombs are more Rococo than Zen. Chosen in 1617 as the burial site of the shogun Ieyasu, Toshogu shrine is a complex of buildings and mausoleums. It is best accessed by the tree-lined avenue leading to Rinno-ji temple, with its thousand-armed Kannon statue and five-storied pagoda. The Yomei-mon gate to Toshogu shrine is lavishly painted and carved. Ieyasu's tomb lies a little higher up a forest path.

② Kawagoe

MAP B1 ▪ Kawagoe, Saitama Prefecture ▪ Tobu Tojo Line from Ikebukuro

Known as "Little Edo," Kawagoe once supplied goods for Edo. Today, the town's main draw is its high street, Ichiban-gai. Many of its traditional warehouses have been converted into stores, galleries, and museums. Yamawa, a ceramic store inside one of the buildings, is a fine example of the architecture of these fireproof structures. Toki no Kane, a wooden bell tower off the main street, has become a symbol of the town.

③ Railway Museum, Omiya

MAP B1 ▪ JR lines from Ueno ▪ Open 10am–6pm Wed–Mon ▪ Adm ▪ www.railway-museum.jp/en

This interactive museum is devoted to the history of Japan's railways since their inception in 1872. There are 30-odd previously used train engines and carriages on display, and you can play at driving a *shinkansen* (bullet train).

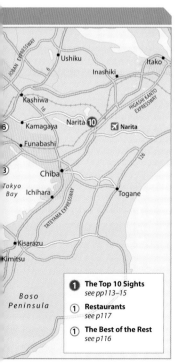

Engines on display, Railway Museum

4 Mount Fuji and Kawaguchi-ko

MAP A2 ■ Express Keio bus from Shinjuku Station ■ mtfuji-jp.com

Sacred Fuji-san, Japan's highest peak, is a beautiful sight close up, particularly in good weather, and the officially active volcano can be seen from the shores of the lakes to its north. The best lake to stay near is Kawaguchi-ko, which has a good range of accommodations and a cable car to the Fuji Viewing Platform.

View of Mount Fuji over a lake

5 Yokohama

MAP B2 ■ Yokohama ■ JR Keihin-Tohoku Line from Tokyo; Minato Mirai subway from Shibuya

A crucial Meiji-era foreign settlement and port, Yokohama includes the Minato Mirai complex, with an art museum, amusement park, stores, and Japan's second-tallest building – Landmark Tower. Moored nearby is a fine old clipper, the *Nippon Maru*. The area offers visitors restaurants and shopping streets of Chinatown, silk and doll museums, old customs buildings, and a lovely Japanese garden, Sankei-en.

6 Hakone

MAP A2 ■ Odakyu express bus from Shinjuku; JR line from Tokyo; Odakyu Line from Shinjuku

The pleasant switchback route up the slopes on the Hakone Tozan Railway starts at Hakone-Yumato, a hot-spring town. Alight at Miyanoshita, stopping for tea at the Fujiya Hotel (see p133). Farther up, the Hakone

EAST MEETS WEST

On July 8, 1853, Commodore Perry, hoping to open Japan to foreign trade and diplomacy, sailed "black ships" into Edo Bay (see p38). The ritual exchange of gifts that ensued – a bronze temple bell and teapot on the Japanese side, a telegraph machine and daguerreotype camera from the visitors – showed how much progress had bypassed Japan.

Open-Air Museum features sculpture by the likes of Rodin and Henry Moore. Gora is the terminus; take the funicular and cable car to the shore of Lake Ashi, stopping off on the way at Owakudani volcanic valley.

7 Mount Takao

MAP B2 ■ Keio Line from Shinjuku Station ■ www.takaosan-onsen.jp/english

Far easier than climbing Mount Fuji, this Quasi-National park has hiking trails as well as a cable car and chair lifts. Near the summit is the Yakuo-in, an 8th-century temple, which hosts a fire festival on the second Sunday in March. The train station, designed by Kengo Kuma, has an open-air bath to relax in before or after your climb.

8 Edo-Tokyo Open Air Architectural Museum

MAP B1 ■ 3-7-1 Sakuramachi, Koganai-shi ■ 042-388-3300 ■ Musashi Koganei, Chuo Line ■ Open Apr–Sep: 9:30am–5:30pm Tue–Sat; Oct–Mar: 9:30am–4:30pm Tue–Sun ■ Adm ■ www.tatemonoen.jp

Buildings representative of Tokyo during the Edo, Meiji, and later

The fascinating Edo-Tokyo Open Air Architectural Museum

periods have been collected and reassembled in this open-air architectural museum, a branch of the Edo-Tokyo Museum in Ryogoku. The museum's farmhouses, villas, public buildings, and bathhouse are set in the middle of Koganei Park.

Daibutsu Buddha, Kamakura

⑨ Kamakura
MAP B2 ■ JR Yokosuka line from Tokyo, Shimbashi, Shinagawa
The shogun's capital from 1192 to 1333, this seaside town has ancient shrines, gardens, and the Daibutsu Buddha statue. Of its two stations, Kita-Kamakura is close to Engaku-ji temple and the gardens and religious spots of Meigetsu-in. Kamakura Station is near the local craft and food stores along Wakamiya-oji and Komachi streets, and Tsurugaoka Hachiman-gu shrine.

⑩ Naritasan Shinshoji Temple
MAP B1 ■ JR or Keisei trains from Ueno ■ www.naritasan.or.jp/english
Established in 940, this beautifully decorated and atmospheric Buddhist temple is set in extensive grounds. Close to Narita Airport, this large complex is a popular pilgrimage location, approached by an appealing shopping street lined with traditional craft stores and restaurants specializing in *unagi* (eel).

TWO DAYS IN KAMAKURA

▶ **DAY 1**

Exiting at **Kamakura** Station, take Komachi-dori, a street with cafés and specialist stores. Return to the station area and take Wakamiya-oji, a street selling local products. At the end of the road, Tsurugaoka Hachiman-gu, **Kamakura's** premier shrine, is dedicated to the god of war. Back at the entrance, turn left for the Kamakura Museum of National Treasures. Stop for tasty noodles at Nakamura-an, along a narrow lane between Wakamiya-oji and Komachi-dori. Take a bus from the No. 5 stop outside the station to Sugimoto-dera, the area's oldest temple. Across the road, Hokoku-ji temple is perfect for tea at the pavilion. A short walk away, Zuizen-ji is a Zen temple with a 14th-century garden.

DAY 2

Get off at Kita-Kamakura Station and stroll to Engaku-ji temple. Walk over the railroad crossing opposite for Tokei-ji temple. Recross the tracks and walk south to Meigetsu-in temple. Return to the road and stroll south toward the wooden gates of Kencho-ji temple. Stop at Hachi-no-ki Honten next door for *shojin ryori* (Buddhist vegetarian cuisine). Retrace your steps until you see a hiking path sign. Turn left for the Daibutsu, the Great Buddha statue. Follow the road to Hase-dera temple, with a view of the bay and town. Take a streetcar to Kamakura Station at **Hase Station** nearby.

See map on p112–13

The Best of the Rest

1 Gotoh Art Museum
MAP C2 ■ 3-9-25 Kaminoge, Setagaya-ku ■ 5777-8600 ■ Open 10am–5pm Tue–Sun ■ Adm

A private collection of Buddhist calligraphy, painting, and rare scrolls.

2 Nihon Minka-en
MAP B2 ■ 7-1-1 Masugata, Kawasaki ■ 044-922-2181 ■ Open Mar–Oct: 9:30am–5pm; Nov–Feb: 9:30am–4:30pm ■ Adm ■ english.nihonminkaen.jp

Traditional farmhouses, merchant homes, tools, and domestic utensils make up this open-air folk museum.

3 Tokyo Disney Resort®
MAP B2 ■ 1-1 Maihama, Urayasu, Chiba Prefecture ■ 045-330-5211 ■ Open times vary, check website ■ Adm ■ www.tokyodisneyresort.jp

Kids will love the popular attractions at Disneyland® and DisneySea®.

4 Hara Museum of Contemporary Art
MAP C2 ■ 4-7-25 Kita-Shinagawa, Shinagawa-ku ■ 3445-0651 ■ Open 11am–5pm Tue–Sun (to 8pm Wed) ■ Adm ■ www.haramuseum.or.jp

Located in a 1939 Bauhaus-style home, this quirky museum has a pleasant sculpture garden and café.

5 Inokashira Park
MAP B2 ■ 1-18-31 Gotenyama, Musashino ■ 0422-47-6900

A popular cherry blossom-viewing venue in early April. On weekends, musicians, market stalls, and street artists take over its paths.

Boating at Inokashira Park

6 Shibamata
MAP B1

Location of the film series *Otoko wa Tsurai Yo* (It's Tough Being a Man), this eastern Tokyo neighborhood has retro charm. Its main shopping street leads to Taishakuten temple.

7 Museum of Contemporary Art (MOT)
MAP C2 ■ 4-1-1 Miyoshi, Koto-ku ■ 5633-5860 ■ Open 10am–6pm Tue–Sun ■ Adm ■ www.mot-art-museum.jp/eng

Next to Kiba Park, this large, modern museum displays post-1945 art from Japan and overseas.

8 Suginami Animation Museum
MAP B1 ■ 3-29-5 Kamiogi, Suginami-ku ■ 3396-1510 ■ Open 10am–6pm Tue–Sun ■ www.sam.or.jp

Kids and Japanese animation fans will appreciate this free museum with displays devoted to the history of anime and some of its most beloved characters.

9 Ghibli Museum
MAP B1 ■ 1-1-83 Shimorenjaku, Mitaka ■ 0570-055-777 ■ Open 10am–6pm Wed–Mon ■ Adm (advance ticket only) ■ www.ghibli-museum.jp

Attracts admirers of the work of animator Hayao Miyazaki.

10 Nakano
MAP C1

Three stops west on the Chuo Line from Shinjuku, Nakano is known for its 1960s shopping strip with stores specializing in anime and manga.

Restaurants

 Heichinro Yokohama Honten

MAP B2 ▪ 149 Yamashita-cho, Naka-ku, Yokohama ▪ 045-681-3001 ▪ ¥¥

Set amidst Yokohama's Chinatown district, this oldest operating Chinese restaurant offers delectable dim sums, and impeccable service.

2 Mutekiro

MAP B2 ▪ 2-96 Motomachi, Naka-ku, Yokohama ▪ 045-681-2926 ▪ ¥¥

Exquisite French food, with a little French pomp thrown in, is the main draw of this place. Set in Yokohama's fashionable Motomachi district, this is a great spot for a romantic meal.

3 Matsubara-an

MAP B2 ▪ 4-10-3 Yuigahama, Kamakura ▪ 0467-61-3838 ▪ ¥¥

Fine soba noodles and other dishes are served in a lovely wooden house in a quiet part of Kamakura. In good weather, there's seating in its garden.

4 Gentoan

MAP B2 ▪ 823 Yamanouchi, Kamakura ▪ 0467-43-5695 ▪ ¥¥

Beyond Gentoan's attractive stone entryway await kaiseki ryori dishes that are so perfectly presented it seems a crime to devour them.

5 Meguri

MAP B1 ▪ 909-1 Nakahatsuishi-machi, Nikko ▪ 0288-25-3122 ▪ Closed Thu & Fri ▪ ¥

Arrive at opening time to be sure of scoring one of the limited number of delicious vegetarian lunches served at this rustic café located on Nikko's main road.

6 Shin-Yokohama Ramen Museum

MAP B2 ▪ 2-14-21 Shin-Yokohama, Kohoku-ku ▪ 045-471-0503 ▪ ¥

The history of Japanese noodles is upstaged by the basement restaurant selling Japan's favorite ramen from Hokkaido to Kyushu.

Restaurant at the Fujiya Hotel

7 Fujiya Hotel

MAP A2 ▪ 359 Miyanoshita ▪ 0460-82-2211 ▪ ¥¥

Waitresses in old-fashioned aprons serve delicious Western dishes in a setting that has changed little since the hotel opened in 1878.

8 Gyoshintei

MAP B1 ▪ 2339-1 Sannai, Nikko ▪ 0288-53-3751 ▪ ¥¥

Buddhist vegetarian and kaiseki-ryori dishes come with lovely views of moss and pine trees in a park-like setting.

9 Bashamichi Taproom

MAP B2 ▪ 5-63-1 Sumiyoshicho, Yokohama ▪ 045-264-4961 ▪ ¥¥

A real-deal American South barbecue, with smoked meats slow-cooked over a cherrywood fire until rich and succulent.

10 Ichinoya

MAP B2 ▪ 1-18-10 Matsuecho, Kawagoe ▪ 049-222-0354 ▪ ¥¥

Traditional eel dishes, a Kawagoe specialty, are served here on a bed of rice along with miso soup and a dish of pickles.

See map on p112–13

Streetsmart

A colorful street in Chinatown, Yokohama

Getting To and Around Tokyo

Arriving by Air

Many airlines, including the national airline JAL (Japan Airlines) and ANA (All Nippon Airways), fly into **Narita International Airport**, (41 miles) 66 km east of central Tokyo, from overseas. **Haneda Airport**, (12 miles) 20 km south of Tokyo, also has a growing number of international connections.

The fastest way into Tokyo from Narita is on the **Keisei Skyliner**, which takes 41 minutes to reach Ueno, where you can connect with the JR Yamanote Line or subways. **Japan Railways (JR)** also runs frequent Narita Express (N'EX) services to Tokyo (53 minutes). Visitors can buy a discount return N'EX ticket valid for 14 days.

Haneda Airport is connected to the city center by both the **Tokyo Monorail** (15 minutes to Hamamatsucho) and the **Keikyu** train line (13 minutes to Shinagawa).

The **Airport Limousine Bus** runs between Narita and Haneda airports to major Tokyo train stations and hotels. See the website for details of discounts for foreign tourists.

A taxi from Narita to central Tokyo will cost you around ¥30,000 while one from Haneda will be around ¥7000.

Arriving by Train

Japan Railways (JR) is the country's principal train operator and it runs the high-speed *shinakansen* (bullet train) services that radiate out from the capital's Tokyo, Ueno, and Shinagawa stations.

If traveling to and from destinations closer to Tokyo, there's competition from other private rail companies such as **Tobu Tojo** to Nikko, **Keisei** to Narita, **Seibu** to Saitama, and **Odakyu** to Hakone.

Arriving by Road

Long-distance buses connect Tokyo with many cities and towns around Japan and can be a very economical way of traveling. Overnight services from Kyoto and Osaka arrive at the Yaesu exit of Tokyo Station; other buses arrive at Ikebukuro Shibuya, Shinagawa, and Shinjuku. The main bus companies are run by JR and **Willer Express**, which offers a Japan Bus Pass (from ¥10,000 for 3 days of unlimited travel).

Arriving by Boat

Long-distance ferries into Tokyo are rare but there are a few services connecting the city with Tokushima in Shikoku and Kita-Kyushu in Kyushu. Ferries and cruise ships dock either at the Harumi Passenger Terminal or Takeshiba Passenger Terminal, which is on the **Yurikamome Line**.

Tokyo has an extensive system of rivers and canals. **Tokyo Cruise** and **Tokyo Mizube Cruising Line** run water-bus services between Asakusa's Azuma Bridge, Hama Rikyu Garden, and Odaiba. Tokyo Cruise also stops at Hinode Pier, while some of Tokyo Mizube's services go out to Kasai Rinkai Park on the east side of Tokyo Bay.

Traveling by Train

Three main JR lines serve Tokyo. The Yamanote Line (green) runs around central Tokyo and includes all the major stations, which serve as departure points for long-distance travel. The Chuo Line (orange) connects Shinjuku and the western suburbs and Tokyo stations, while the Sobu Line (yellow) also connects Shinjuku to the eastern suburbs.

The **Yurikamome Line** connects Shimbashi with Toyosu (both on Tokyo's subway system) and is the main way to travel around the island of Odaiba.

Traveling by Subway

There are 13 lines in Tokyo, nine run by **Tokyo Metro**, four by **Toei**. The system is color-coded, but the number of stations and intersecting points can be daunting. Station subway maps in English are available in tourist offices or you can download the **Navitime for Japan Travel** app.

Traveling by Monorail and Tram

Tokyo Monorail connects Haneda Airport with Hamamatsucho Station (on the JR Yamanote Line). The last of Tokyo's city-operated streetcar services is the Toden Arakawa Line, which is run by Toei.

Traveling by Bus

Tokyo is served by many bus companies; most have digital signage that switches between English and Japanese. Each trip is ¥210, which can be paid in cash, or you can use prepaid smart cards.

Traveling by Public Transport

Smart cards, **Suica** and **Pasmo**, can be bought from vending machines at most train and subway stations. They are valid on all Tokyo transport. For travel outside Tokyo, the **Japan Rail Pass** covers the entire JR network, but you must purchase this before traveling to Japan.

Traveling by Car

Driving around Tokyo is not a good idea. Traffic jams are common, and missing a turn can prove disastrous. International Driving Permit is required to rent a car. Companies such as **Nippon Rent-a-Car** and **Toyota Rent-a-Car** offer good service.

Traveling by Taxi

Taxis fares are expensive, starting at around ¥730. Fares are higher on weekends and between 11pm and 5am. Taxi stands are found near all stations, department stores, and big hotels. **Nihon Kotsu** and **Hinomaru Limousine** are reliable service providers.

Traveling by Bicycle

As long as you avoid the major roads, it can be a delight cycling around Tokyo's quieter streets and back alleys. There are several rental bike services such as **Cogi Cogi** and **Rent a Bike**. Around 150 free bicycles are available every Sunday between 10am and 3pm near Nijubashimae Station for a circuit of the Imperial Palace moats.

DIRECTORY

ARRIVING BY AIR

Airport Limousine Bus
limousinebus.co.jp/en

Haneda Airport
haneda-airport.jp/inter/en

Narita International Airport
narita-airport.jp/en/index.html

ARRIVING BY TRAIN

Japan Railways (JR)
jreast.co.jp/e

Keikyu Trains
haneda-tokyo-access.com/en

Keisei
keisei.co.jp

Keisei Skyliner
keisei.co.jp/keisei/tetudou/skyliner/us

Odakyu
odakyu.jp/english

Seibu
seiburailway.jp/railways/tourist/english

Tobu
tobu.co.jp/foreign/index.html

ARRIVING BY ROAD

Willer Express
willerexpress.com/en

ARRIVING BY BOAT

Tokyo Cruise
suijobus.co.jp

Tokyo Mizube Cruising Line
tokyo-park.or.jp/waterbus/english/index.html

TRAVELING BY SUBWAY

Navitime for Japan Travel
navitime.co.jp

Toei
kotsu.metro.tokyo.jp/eng

Tokyo Metro
tokyometro.jp/en

Yurikamome Line
yurikamome.co.jp

TRAVELING BY MONORAIL AND TRAM

Tokyo Monorail
tokyo-monorail.co.jp/english

TRAVELING BY PUBLIC TRANSPORT

Japan Rail Pass
japan-rail-pass.com

Pasmo
pasmo.co.jp/en

Suica
jreast.co.jp/e/pass/suica.html

TRAVELING BY CAR

Nippon Rent-a-Car
nipponrentacar.co.jp

Toyota Rent-a-Car
rent.toyota.co.jp

TRAVELING BY TAXI

Hinomaru Limousine
hinomaruny.com

Nihon Kotsu
nihon-kotsu.co.jp

TRAVELING BY BICYCLE

Cogi Cogi
cogicogi.jp

Rent a Bike
rentabike.jp

Practical Information

Passports and Visas

A 90-day visitor visa is issued on arrival to citizens of Western countries as well as of Singapore, South Korea, and Hong Kong. Visa extension requests can be made at the Immigration Bureau at least 10 days before the original visa expires. The website of the **Japan Ministry of Foreign Affairs** has a guide to Japanese visas.

Most countries have consular representation in Tokyo, including the **USA**, **Ireland**, **Australia**, **New Zealand**, and the **UK**.

Customs and Immigration

Landing forms and passports are required at immigration gates. All foreign nationals are fingerprinted before entering the country. Unless you are exceeding the duty-free limit, no detailed list of your belongings is necessary. There are no restrictions on the amount of incoming currency allowed.

Travel Safety Advice

Visitors can get up-to-date travel safety information from the **Foreign and Commonwealth Office** in the UK, the **State Department** in the US, and the **Department of Foreign Affairs and Trade** in Australia.

Travel Insurance

All travelers are advised to buy insurance against theft or loss, accidents, illness, and travel delays or cancellations. As a visitor, you will be expected to pay the full amount for any health treatments. Charges for consultations and drugs are high. Be sure to carry proof of health insurance.

Health

Do not rely on hospitals and clinics to have English-speaking staff. Exceptions include the **Japan Red Cross Medical Center**, **Hiroo Hospital**, and **St Luke's International Hospital**.

Dental problems are more self-explanatory than medical ones, so the shortage of English-speaking dentists is not a major problem. Hotel staff can make a recommendation, contact a local clinic, and provide a note in Japanese explaining the problem. The **Tokyo Clinic Dental Office** has English-speaking staff.

Tokyo has a surfeit of well-stocked pharmacies, although the staff may not speak English. The **American Pharmacy** in the basement of the Marunouchi Building on Marunouchi's Naka-dori, however, has English-speaking staff.

Personal Security

Tokyo is subject to frequent tremors, although most are minor. Earthquake drills take place every September 1, the anniversary of the quake that devastated Tokyo in 1923. If you're inside, the best advice in the event of a quake is to crouch under a heavy table. Make sure all doors are open and gas appliances switched off.

Tokyo remains one of the safest cities in the world with crimes such as muggings and violent attacks very rare. However, care should be taken while walking in some crowded areas, such as Kabukicho and Roppongi. Hotel staff are scrupulously honest.

With a relatively low crime rate, assaults on women travelers are also rare. Drunken men can be annoying, but rarely threatening; ignoring them is usually the best course. That said, sexual harassment on trains has been serious enough for some train companies to introduce women-only carriages during the rush hours. Some hotels exist exclusively for women.

Emergency Services

If you have problems getting the **Ambulance**, **Fire**, and **Police** emergency services to understand your call, there is an **Emergency Interpretation** service. The **Japan Helpline** and **Tokyo Foreign Residents Advisory Service** can also be useful; both are staffed by English speakers.

Travelers with Specific Needs

Tokyo is not the easiest city for travelers with specific needs to negotiate, though new buildings and developments have ramps installed.

Lines of yellow raised dots on the ground guide the visually impaired, and traffic lights have audible signals for crossing. Trains have special seats, and many ticket machines have Braille plates.

Go online for obtaining information about the following organizations: **Accessible Japan, Japan Accessible Tourism Center**, and **Japanese Red Cross Language Service Volunteers**.

Currency and Banking

Yen banknotes have four denominations: ¥10,000, ¥5,000, ¥2,000 (rarely seen), and ¥1,000. Coins are found in units of ¥500, ¥100, ¥50, ¥10, ¥5, and ¥1. Check exchange rates against your own currency before you travel. For day-to-day banking needs, there are numerous international banks to choose from, such as Sumitomo Mitsui, and Mizuho banks. Most banks are open from 9am to 3pm on weekdays.

Tokyo-Mitsubishi UFJ bank (MUFG) runs World Currency Shop foreign exchange counters in major shopping centers. Foreign currencies can be changed and travelers' checks cashed at authorized foreign exchange banks. Some stores and hotels change money and travelers' checks.

Very few standard ATMs accept foreign-issued cards. One exception is Japan Post Bank where the operational hours of the ATM depend on the opening hours of the post office branch. ATMs at 7–Eleven convenience stores also accept foreign credit and debit cards. ATMs usually give a slightly better exchange rate than exchanging cash or travelers' checks in department stores and hotels.

Although the Japanese still prefer using cash, many hotels, department stores and large restaurants accept credit cards. American Express, Diners Club, MasterCard, and Visa are widely accepted.

DIRECTORY

PASSPORTS AND VISAS

Australia
🆆 japan.embassy.gov.au

Ireland
🆆 dfa.ie/irish-embassy/japan

Japan Ministry of Foreign Affairs
🆆 mofa.go.jp

New Zealand
🆆 mfat.govt.nz

UK
🆆 gov.uk/government/world/organisations/british-embassy-tokyo

USA
🆆 japan.usembassy.gov

TRAVEL SAFETY ADVICE

Australia Department of Foreign Affairs and Trade
🆆 dfat.gov.au
🆆 smartraveller.gov.au

UK Foreign and Commonwealth Office
🆆 gov.uk/foreign-travel-advice

US Department of State
🆆 travel.state.gov

HEALTH

American Pharmacy
📞 5220-7716

Hiroo Hospital
📞 3444-1181
🆆 byouin.metro.tokyo.jp

Japan Red Cross Medical Center
📞 3400-1311
🆆 med.jrc.or.jp

St Luke's International Hospital
📞 3541-5151
🆆 hospital.luke.ac.jp/eng

Tokyo Clinic Dental Office
📞 3431-4225
🆆 tcdo.jp

EMERGENCY SERVICES

Ambulance and Fire
📞 119

Police
📞 110

Emergency Interpretation
🆆 himawari.metro.tokyo.jp/qq/qq13tomnlt.asp

Japan Helpline
📞 0120-46-1997

Tokyo Foreign Residents Advisory Service
🆆 metro.tokyo.jp/ENGLISH/GUIDE/guide01.html

TRAVELERS WITH SPECIFIC NEEDS

Accessible Japan
🆆 accessible-japan.com

Japan Accessible Tourism Center
🆆 japan-accessible.com

Japanese Red Cross Language Service Volunteers
🆆 tok-lanserv.jp/eng

Telephone and Internet

With the exception of train stations and some convenience stores, public phones are a rarity. Some phones accept international credit cards. Buy telephone cards from the big telecom companies, such as NTT and KDDI, which you can get at convenience stores.

Japan doesn't have a GSM mobile phone system so GSM-only mobile phones will not work here. Modern 3G and 4G phones will, but you must either have international roaming enabled on the device, or rent or buy a prepaid SIM card from a Japanese operator, such as **DoCoMo** and **Softbank Telecom**.

There are vending machines selling pre-paid data-only SIMs at Narita Airport and Aqua City mall in Odaiba. Smart phones will also allow you to make calls via Wi-Fi using Skype or similar VOIP apps.

It is possible to rent a cell phone at provider service desks at Narita and Haneda airports or via **Rentafone Japan**, which can post the phone to your accommodation.

Etiquette requires people to switch off their cell phones while they are in temples, gardens, and restaurants, though it is often ignored.

Major railway stations (all Yamanote Line and many *shinkansen* stations), international airports, hotels, restaurants, convenience store chains, and tourist information centers offer free internet access and Wi-Fi.

Postal Services

Yubin-kyoku (post offices) bear red signs resembling a "T." Mail boxes, too, are red. Post office hours are usually from 9am to 5pm on weekdays. Some main offices open on Saturdays from 9am to 12:30pm. Express mail services, such as EMS, are reliable. Send priority mail from the Tokyo International Post Office and Tokyo Central Post, each with all-night counters.

Television and Radio

The state broadcaster **NHK** has two local and two satellite TV channels. Tokyo has five other local channels. Satellite service **SkyPerfecTV!** has a huge range of channels. **InterFM** broadcasts music and news.

Newspapers and Magazines

The daily English-language newspaper **The Japan Times** has the best local news coverage and international reportage, as well as useful information about what's going on in Tokyo. You will also be able to find local news online at **Japan Today** and the **Asahi Shimbun**.

The free monthly **Metropolis** magazine features art, culture, and entertainment listings in Tokyo, as well as feature stories. **Tokyo Weekender** has good Tokyo listings, with features on Japan.

Opening Hours

General opening hours for shops are from 10am to 8pm daily, but you'll find many convenience stores also open 24 hours. Restaurants serve lunch between 11.30am and 2.30pm and dinner from 6pm to 10pm, with last orders taken usually an hour before closing. Bars open around 5pm and close in the early hours of the morning. Banks are open 9am to 3pm Monday to Friday, with some open until 8pm. Museums open at 9am or 10am and close around 5pm, with last entry usually an hour before that; most museums and galleries are closed on Monday.

Time Difference

Tokyo time is 9 hours ahead of GMT and 14 hours ahead of US EST. There is no daylight-savings time.

Electrical Appliances

Japan uses a two-pin plug common in Asia and North America. The current is 100V AC. Tokyo and the eastern part of Japan are on the 50Hz system. Adaptors are sold at electric stores all across Tokyo.

Weather

Crisp days in winter (Dec–Feb) can be pleasant. Temperatures occasionally drop below zero, but snow is rare. Spring (Apr–May) is generally mild, with some rainfall in late April.

The summer months (Jun–late Sep) can be stiflingly hot, with temperatures rising to 100°F (38°C). June to mid-July is the rainy season, with high humidity.

Typhoons may hit the city in September and October, but these are unpredictable. Temperatures drop in fall (Nov), but the skies are clear and the trees are beautifully colorful.

Spring and fall are the best months for outdoor festivals and cultural events. Golden Week (Apr 29–May 5) and the New Year (Dec 28–Jan 4) are major vacations, when there is a stiff rise in flight and accommodation costs.

Visitor Information

There are several useful Tourist Information Centers (TICs) in Tokyo and at both international airports including **TIC Tokyo**, where you should be able to find staff who speak English as well as other languages. These centers can provide maps, leaflets, and itineraries, among other services.

At the Marunouchi exit of Tokyo Station, staff at the **JR East Travel Service Center** can also make hotel bookings (not available elsewhere). The **Japan National Tourism Organization (JNTO)** has an information office in the Shin-Tokyo Building on Marunouchi's Naka-dori that's open daily 9am to 5pm. There is also the **Tokyo Tourist Information Center**, which has four locations, one of which is in the Tokyo Metropolitan Government Building in Shinjuku; it is open 9.30am to 6.30pm.

Go Tokyo is the city's official tourism information site, available in English.

Trips and Tours

Gray Line, **SkyBus**, and **Hato Bus Tours** all offer sightseeing bus tours around Tokyo.

If you prefer to see the city on foot, the **Tokyo Metropolitan Government** offers free guided tours out of city hall in Shinjuku. **Tokyo SGG Club** also offers free tours on a first-come, first-served basis.

Walking tours and other cultural experiences can be arranged through **True Japan Tours** and **The Backstreet Guides**, while tours on a bicycle can be taken with **Tokyo Great Cycle Tour**.

To get a bird's-eye view of Tokyo take a helicopter tour, which can be arranged through **Excel Air Services**.

DIRECTORY

TELEPHONE AND INTERNET

DoCoMo
w nttdocomo.co.jp/english

Rentafone Japan
w rentafonejapan.com

Softbank Telecom
w softbank.jp/en

POSTAL SERVICES

Japan Post
w post.japanpost.jp/english

TELEVISION AND RADIO

InterFM
w interfm.co.jp

NHK
w nhk.or.jp

Sky PerfecTV!
w skyperfectv.co.jp/eng

NEWSPAPERS AND MAGAZINES

Asahi Shimbun
w asahi.com/ajw

Japan Times
w japantimes.co.jp

Metropolis
w metropolisjapan.com

Japan Today
w japantoday.com

Tokyo Weekender
w tokyoweekender.com

VISITOR INFORMATION

Go Tokyo
w gotokyo.org/en

Japan National Tourism Organization (JNTO)
c 3201-3331
w jnto.go.jp

JR East Travel Service Center
w jreast.co.jp/e/customer_support/service_center_tokyo.html

TIC Tokyo
w tictokyo.jp/en
c 5220-7055

Tokyo Tourist Information Center
c 5321-3077

TRIPS AND TOURS

Excel Air Services
w excel-air.com/english

Gray Line
w jgl.co.jp/inbound

Hato Bus Tours
w hatobus.com/int/en

SkyBus
w skybus.jp

The Backstreet Guides
w thebackstreetguides.com

Tokyo Great Cycle Tour
w tokyocycling.jp

Tokyo Metropolitan Government Walking Tours
w gotokyo.org/en/tourists/guideservice/guideservice/index.html

Tokyo SGG Club
w tokyosgg.jp

True Japan Tours
w truejapantours.com

Shopping

In Tokyo, consumer culture options are everywhere, and the city excels at both fashion and food.

Consumption tax, currently 8 percent, will rise to 10 percent in October 2019. Many department stores and electrical goods stores in places such as Akihabara offer tax exemptions for purchases over ¥10,000. After paying, take the goods, your receipts, and passport to the tax-refund counter for reimbursement. **JNTO** has a page on tax-free shopping on its website.

Tokyo's fashion districts tend to be generational. Ginza and Aoyama attract a middle-aged, well-heeled crowd, though some stores such as Uniqlo have been making a bid for the youth market. Harajuku appeals to mid-teens, Shibuya to high-teens to those in their early 20s, Shimokitazawa to the college crowd, and Naka-Meguro and Daikanyama to 20- and 30-somethings.

Akihabara, or "Akiba" as it is called, is the world's largest electronic center, stocking everything from portable music units to robot pets and toys, all at very competitive prices. It's also the main area to shop for items related to anime and manga, along with Ikebukuro and Nakano. Large electronics stores such as Bic Camera and Yodobashi Camera can be found close to other major Yamanote line stations.

Tokyo's department stores (*depato*) are a great shopping experience. Typically, the first floors sell women's clothing and accessories, with menswear on the floor above. Stores are lifestyle complexes, places where people stop for coffee or lunch, to relax in a rooftop beer garden, to take in an exhibition, or join a culture class. The stores also sell tickets for concerts and exhibitions.

For English-language books and magazines, the main bookshops to head to are **Maruzen** in the Oazu complex in Marunouchi and **Kinokuniya**'s two stores in Shinjuku.

Tokyo has countless new and used record stores. The **Tower Records** Shibuya store has six floors of music. Nearby, **HMV** is massive. If there is something you missed the first time round, Shibuya and Shinjuku's used CD and vinyl stores, which include **Recofan** and **Disk Union**, may be the place to find it.

Dining

Every style of Japanese cuisine is available in Tokyo – from prime Kobe steaks and top-class sushi to Buddhist vegetarian cuisine and all kinds of tofu. There are tens of thousands of restaurants and cafés catering to hungry diners: you can stand up and slurp ramen noodles at a hole-in-the-wall bar, or sit down to a splendid multi-course *kaiseki* (Japanese haute cuisine) menu.

Department stores offer a wide range of pastries, Japanese sweets, cured and dried seafood, and wines in their basements. In addition to these, there are counters where one can expect to find dishes such as sushi and *tonkatsu* (deep-fried pork cutlets). Mitsukoshi (see p66) is known for the quality and selection of food items in the basement.

Japanese food is available across the city, and it's usually easy to find restaurants offering all the major European and Asian cuisines too. One of the city's best areas to sample ethnic food is Shin-Okubo, which serves Burmese, Indonesian, Korean, and Malaysian, as well as Nepalese dishes.

Make reservations at top-end restaurants. Those that require advance booking on the phone usually have English-speaking staff. If not, your hotel may be able to help. In most places, the waiter will automatically come for your order. Many restaurants have photo menus and often plastic food displays in the window. Waiters come to your table with the bill, which you take to the cash register to pay. You can place your money on a small dish and the change will be put back on the dish with the receipt. There is no need to leave a tip at hotels, restaurants, in taxis or for any service. In some cases, it is considered rude. A few high-end restaurants may include a 10 percent service charge to bills.

Useful listings websites include **Tokyo Food Page** and **Gurunavi**.

Accommodation

Tokyo's choice of accommodations ranges from five-star luxury hotels to capsule hotels.

Tokyo is a busy city, so it's always wise to book well ahead. Reservations can be especially hard to come by during the three big vacations at New Year's (Dec 25–Jan 4), Golden Week (Apr 29–May 5), and O-Bon (mid-Aug). Rooms can also get booked up in February, when students take their university entrance exams.

There has been a boom in no-frills business-style hotels, such as those offered by the chain **Toyoko Inn**. These are often found close to major train and metro stations. The rooms are functional and the rates include a basic buffet breakfast. **Japan Youth Hostels, Inc** also offers accommodation to budget travelers.

Staying in a traditional Japanese inn is well worth it. The main difference between a *ryokan* and a *minshuku* is like that between a hotel and a B&B, with *minshuku* tending to be more at the budget end of the price range and with the family who run it living on-site. Find your choice at the **Japanese Ryokan & Hotel Association** and **Japanese Inn Group**.

The etiquette for staying at a *ryokan* or *minshuku* is universal. Shoes are removed before entering the inn and exchanged for house slippers. Slippers should be taken off before stepping on the *tatami* mats. A separate pair of slippers is worn in the toilet area. There may be a communal bathroom: if there's just one communal bath, there will be fixed times for male and female bathing. When going to and from the bath, put on the *yukata* (cotton robe) provided. At the finest of *ryokan*, elaborate multi-course meals (both for dinner and breakfast) are included in the rates and often served by staff dressed in kimono, either in your room or a private booth of the restaurant.

Unique Japanese places to stay include capsule hotels and love hotels. Neither are designed for long stays but can be fun to experience for a night.

Capsule hotels offer beds enclosed in oblong cabins that are stacked on top of each other in two tiers. They cater mainly to "salarymen" who have missed their last trains home, so are usually located around major train stations. Most are for men only, but at a few you'll find women-only floors. All the bathing facilities are communal.

Love hotels, on the other hand, are for couples seeking some privacy. They can be rented for an hour "rest" or an overnight "stay". Payment is then made via a machine or to a cashier who sits hidden behind a screen, as the basic theme of all love hotels being privacy.

All hotels charge an 8-percent tax, which most budget and some mid-range places include in the rate. An extra ¥100 tax is charged for rooms over ¥10,000 and ¥200 for those over ¥15,000. High-end hotels include a service charge of 10 to 15 percent.

Useful hotel booking websites include **Japan Hotel Association** and **JAPANiCAN**.

Places to Stay

PRICE CATEGORIES

For a standard, double room per night (with breakfast if included), taxes and extra charges.

¥ under ¥15,000 ¥¥ ¥15,000–35,000 ¥¥¥ over ¥35,000

Luxury Hotels

Aman Tokyo

MAP M2 ■ 1-5-6 Otemachi, Chiyoda-ku ■ 5224-3333 ■ www. aman.com ■ ¥¥¥

At the top of the Otemachi Tower, this luxury chain hotel brings its sophisticated calm and style to Tokyo with a serene spa, a swimming pool with great city views, and traditional Japanese touches to the room decor.

Andaz Hotel

MAP L5 ■ 1-23-4, Toranomon, Minato-ku ■ 6830-1234 ■ www. tokyo.andaz.hyatt.com ■ ¥¥¥

Part of the Toranomon Hills complex, the Andaz offers real glamour and a great location midway between Roppongi and Ginza. The rooms are extremely spacious by Tokyo standards and offer panoramic city views.

Cerulean Tower Tokyu Hotel

MAP R6 ■ 26-1 Sakuragaoka-cho, Shibuya-ku ■ 3476-3000 ■ www.tokyuhotels.co.jp/ cerulean-h ■ ¥¥¥

Shibuya's premier luxury hotel boasts huge rooms, stylish interiors, *kaiseki* restaurants, bars, a jazz club, and a traditional Noh theater. The best rooms for breathtaking views are those between the 13th and 37th floors.

Grand Hyatt Tokyo

MAP C6 ■ 6-10-3 Roppongi, Minato-ku ■ 4333-1234 ■ www. tokyo.grand.hyatt.com ■ ¥¥¥

Luxurious rooms come with top-grade facilities. All the rooms are tastefully decked out with a combination of natural elements and sleek, contemporary furnishings. Also on-site is an excellent selection of restaurants, a fantastic patisserie, and a spa.

Hotel Chinzanso

MAP D1 ■ 2-10-8 Sekiguchi, Bunkyo-ku ■ 3943-1111 ■ www.hotel-chinzanso-tokyo.com ■ ¥¥¥

The lobby and corridors of this opulent hotel are decorated with original artwork. Its magnificent Japanese garden has some original features, including a wooden pagoda and Buddhist stone statuary. Rooms are immaculate.

Hotel New Otani Tokyo

MAP D4 ■ 4-1 Kioi-cho, Chiyoda-ku ■ 3265-1111 ■ www.newotani.co.jp ■ ¥¥¥

Business tycoons, rock stars, and diplomats have stayed in this colossal hotel, which resembles a mini-city within the megalopolis. Lavishly furnished rooms and beautifully landscaped Japanese gardens add to the elegance. The 17th-floor rotating restaurant offers splendid views.

Hotel Okura Tokyo

MAP K5 ■ 2-10-4 Toranomon, Minato-ku ■ 3582-0111 ■ www. hotelokura.co.jp/tokyo/en ■ ¥¥¥

Okura's main building has been reconstructed for the 2020 Olympics. This iconic hotel has excellent service. The lobby here sports a retro style, and the rooms are spacious and comfortable.

Imperial Hotel

MAP M4 ■ 1-1-1 Uchisaiwaicho, Chiyoda-ku ■ 3504-1111 ■ www.imperialhotel. co.jp ■ ¥¥¥

With a history dating from the 1890s, the Imperial Hotel boasts excellent credentials. Rooms on the Imperial Floor are slightly larger and have the most up-to-date decor. The Imperial's location is also very good: it is set just across from Hibiya Park (see p81) and a short stroll away from Ginza.

Mandarin Oriental Tokyo

MAP N2 ■ 2-1-1 Nihonbashi-Muromachi, Chuo-ku ■ 3270-8800 ■ www.mandarinoriental. com/tokyo ■ ¥¥¥

The Mandarin Oriental oozes luxury. Japanese artisan materials, such as paper lanterns, hanging textiles, and traditional furnishings. Panoramic views of Mount Fuji and the Tokyo business district add to the charm. There are also several exceptional bars and restaurants on-site.

Palace Hotel

MAP M2 ▪ 1-1-1 Marunouchi, Chiyoda-ku ▪ 3211-5211 ▪ en.palace hoteltokyo.com ▪ ¥¥¥

Given a makeover in 2012, this is a serenely quiet, classic establishment with spacious rooms. Counting the Japanese emperor as a neighbor, the Palace Hotel also offers great views of the Imperial Palace (see pp12–13).

Park Hyatt Tokyo

MAP A4 ▪ 3-7-1-2 Nishi-Shinjuku, Shinjuku-ku ▪ 5322-1234 ▪ www. tokyo.park.hyatt.com ▪ ¥¥¥

The hotel was the setting for the Scarlett Johansson movie *Lost in Translation*. It offers stellar views, especially at night. The spa and the magnificent swimming pool are in a class of their own. Expect superb service and first-class bars and restaurants.

Peninsula Hotel Tokyo

MAP M4 ▪ 1-8-1 Yurakucho, Chiyoda-ku ▪ 6270-2888 ▪ www.tokyo. peninsula.com ▪ ¥¥¥

Completed in 2008, this reputed 24-story hotel overlooks both the Imperial Palace East Gardens (see p12) and Hibiya Park (see p50). Shopping in Ginza and Marunouchi is a short stroll away.

Ritz-Carlton

MAP D5 ▪ Tokyo Midtown, 9-7-1 Akasaka, Minato-ku ▪ 3423-8000 ▪ www.ritz carlton.com ▪ ¥¥¥

Set close to the heart of the Roppongi entertainment area, the sumptuous Ritz-Carlton has spell-binding views, outstanding bars and restaurants, and world-class amenities. As you would expect of a hotel of this class, the service is second to none.

Shangri-La Hotel

MAP N3 ▪ Marunouchi Trust Tower Main, 1-8-3 Marunouchi, Chiyoda-ku ▪ 6739-7888 ▪ www. shangri-la.com ▪ ¥¥¥

Located next to Tokyo Station, the Shangri-La offers guests handsomely appointed rooms that look out over striking cityscape vistas. Visitors will find impeccable service here, plus excellent facilities.

The Strings by InterContinental Tokyo

MAP C2 ▪ Shinagawa East One Tower, 26-32F, 2-16-1 Konan, Minato-ku ▪ 5783-1111 ▪ www.interconti nental-strings.jp ▪ ¥¥¥

Spread across the 26th to 32nd floors, the hotel has scenic views of Odaiba Island (see pp34–5) and Rainbow Bridge (see p34). The rooms are flooded with natural light thanks to their large windows and feature modern furniture in muted colors, with comfortable low-slung sofas.

Mid-Range Hotels

Claska

MAP C2 ▪ 1-3-18 Chuo-cho, Meguro-ku ▪ 3719-8121 ▪ www.claska.com ▪ ¥¥

The slightly inconvenient location is worth it to experience this two-floor hotel's ultra-modern design style. All rooms are spacious. The hotel also has a gallery, bookstore, and restaurant-bar.

Granbell Hotel

MAP B6 ▪ 15-17 Sakuragaoka-cho, Shibuya-ku ▪ 5457-2681 ▪ www.granbellhotel.jp ▪ ¥¥

This cheerful hotel is a short walk from Shibuya Station. Double and single rooms have simple furnishings. There is also an excellent, but expensive, maisonette-style terrace suite.

Hilltop Hotel

MAP E3 ▪ 1-1 Kanda-Surugadai, Chiyoda-ku ▪ 3293-2311 ▪ www. yamanoue-hotel.co.jp ▪ ¥¥

An old favorite with Tokyo writers, this pre-war Art Deco hotel exudes charm and character. The older rooms are furnished with old-fashioned writing desks, while the more expensive suites have small private gardens.

Hotel Ginza Premier

MAP M5 ▪ 8-13-1 Ginza, Chuo-ku ▪ 3543-1131 ▪ www.gardenhotels. co.jp ▪ ¥¥

Located in Ginza, this modern skyscraper hotel offers four-star luxury and beautiful views at a reasonable price. There are other Mitsui Garden hotels nearby.

Hotel Monterey Hanzomon

MAP K2 ▪ 23-1 Ichibancho, Chiyoda-ku ▪ 3556-7111 ▪ www. hotelmonterey.co.jp ▪ ¥¥

The rooms here blend contemporary architecture with traditional Japanese design, while the wall colors reflect the tastes of samurai residences of the Edo period. There are three other equally good Monterey hotels in Tokyo.

For a key to hotel price categories see p128

Hotel Niwa Tokyo

MAP E3 ▪ 1-1-16 Kanda-Misakicho, Chiyoda-ku ▪ 3293-0028 ▪ www.hotelniwa.jp/en ▪ ¥¥

For a bargain price, this central hotel has much to offer, including a rooftop garden and two restaurants. The good-sized rooms boast modern Japanese decor; some also have balconies and city views.

Hotel S

MAP C6 ▪ 1-11-6 Nishi-Azabu, Minato-ku ▪ 5771-2469 ▪ www.hr-roppongi.jp/en ▪ ¥¥

A fun option that suits the nightlife vibe of the area, Hotel S's boutique-style rooms come in a range of individual themes from zen simplicity to duplexes with grassy colored and textured carpets.

Keio Plaza Hotel

MAP A4 ▪ 2-2-1 Nishi-Shinjuku, Shinjuku-ku ▪ 3344-0111 ▪ www.keioplaza.co.jp ▪ ¥¥

One of the best bases for visiting the sights of Shinjuku. Room rates here are reasonable, given its location among the skyscrapers of West Shinjuku and its first-rate amenities, including several restaurants, stores, and an outdoor pool.

Budget Hotels

Asia Center of Japan

MAP C5 ▪ 8-10-32 Akasaka, Minato-ku ▪ 3402-6111 ▪ www.asiacenter.or.jp ▪ ¥

In the heart of fashionable Aoyama, the Asia Center offers all the facilities of a business hotel at affordable rates. Rooms are basic but reasonably spacious. A free buffet breakfast is available to overseas guests and staff all speak English.

Khaosan Tokyo Laboratory

MAP Q3 ▪ 2-1-4 Nishi-Asakusa, Taito-ku ▪ 6479-1041 ▪ www.khaosan-tokyo.com/en/laboratory ▪ ¥

Perfect for families with young kids, this hostel has a range of vividly painted rooms with a double and single bed, as well as dorms sleeping four, all of which have en suite bathrooms.

K's House Tokyo

MAP R3 ▪ 3-20-10 Kuramae, Taito-ku ▪ 5833-0555 ▪ www.kshouse.jp/tokyo-e ▪ ¥

Set in a yellow-painted building a short walk south of Asakusa, this comfortable hostel has a mix of dorms and private rooms, a roof terrace, and a pleasant lounge, where you can hang out and meet fellow travelers.

Nui

MAP R3 ▪ 2-14-13 Kuramae, Taito-ku ▪ 6240-9854 ▪ www.backpackers japan.co.jp/nuihostel/english.html ▪ ¥

From the Toco team comes this hip hostel in a converted warehouse. High-ceilinged dormitories and private rooms share the communal bathrooms while on the ground floor is a popular café-bar that attracts the area's creatives.

Retrometro Backpackers

MAP Q2 ▪ 2-19-1 Nishi-Asakusa, Taito-ku ▪ 6322-7447 ▪ ¥

An appealing hostel set in a converted old wooden house located in Asakusa, Retrometro offers just two compact dorms and is run by an experienced Japanese traveler who knows how to make her guests feel at home. A stylish establishment with a serene vibe.

Sakura Hotel

MAP L1 ▪ 2-21-4 Kanda-Jimbocho, Chiyoda-ku ▪ 3261-3939 ▪ www.sakura-hotel.co.jp ▪ ¥

A popular choice with budget-range travelers, the Sakura Hotel offers accommodation options comprising shared dorms and minuscule, but cozy, private rooms, all non-smoking. The English-speaking staff are very friendly, and the hotel's good location is a bonus.

Shinjuku Kuyakusho-mae Capsule Hotel

MAP B3 ▪ 1-2-5 Kabukicho, Shinjuku-ku ▪ 3232-1110 ▪ www.hgpshinjuku.jp/en ▪ ¥

Offering perfect access to the Shinjuku area, this inexpensive, clean capsule hotel is just a four minute walk from the station. There are separate capsule floors for men and women.

Toco

MAP G1 ▪ 2-13-21 Shitaya, Taito-ku ▪ 6458-1686 ▪ www.backpackers japan.co.jp ▪ ¥

A geisha used to live in this lovely 1920s wooden building, which has been converted into a cool hostel. There are small dorms and a handful of private Japanese-style rooms. The hostel also has a serene Japanese garden and pleasant lounge bar.

Tokyo Central Youth Hostel

MAP B3 ■ Central Plaza 18F, 1-1 Kaguragashi, Shinjuku-ku ■ 3235-1107 ■ www.jyh.gr.jp/tcyh/e/top.html ■ ¥

A modern hostel on the 18th and 19th floors of Central Plaza. Except for a Japanese-style family room, accommodation is in shared dorms. Other features include a souvenir store, dining hall, Internet access, and a TV in the lobby.

Tokyo Hütte

MAP D1 ■ 4-18-16 Narihira, Sumida-ku ■ 5637-7628 ■ www.tokyohutte.co.jp/en/ ■ ¥

Across the Sumida River (see pp16–17) from the district of Asakusa and within a stone's throw of Tokyo Skytree (see p89) is this stylish new hostel. The mixed and female-only dorms offer extra-wide beds screened off by curtains to ensure privacy and there are private Japanese-style rooms. Communal bathroom.

Rooms with a View

Asakusa View Hotel

MAP Q2 ■ 3-17-1 Nishi-Asakusa, Taito-ku ■ 3847-1111 ■ www.viewhotels.co.jp/asakusa/english ■ ¥¥

As the name suggests, the views of neighboring rooftops and the nearby Senso-ji temple (see pp14–15) from these comfortable Western-style rooms are of a charming older Tokyo. The bar on the 28th floor offers visitors the best views of the Sumida River and the nearby Tokyo Skytree tower.

Hilton Tokyo Odaiba

MAP D2 ■ 1-9-1 Daiba, Minato-ku ■ 5500-5500 ■ www3.hilton.com ■ ¥¥

This well-appointed hotel is located next to the Tokyo Decks mall, near the Odaiba Marine Park (see p35) with its man-made beach and copy of the Statue of Liberty. Its luxurious rooms offer stunning vistas of the bay, island, and waterfront.

Hotel Park Side

MAP F2 ■ 2-11-18 Ueno, Taito-ku ■ 3836-5711 ■ www.parkside.co.jp ■ ¥¥

This good-value hotel offers Japanese- and Western-style rooms. Rooms on the middle to upper floors have the finest views of Ueno Park and its lotus pond, which is at its best in summer.

InterContinental Tokyo Bay

MAP C1 ■ 1-16-2 Kaigan, Minato-ku ■ 5404-2222 ■ www.interconti-tokyo.com ■ ¥¥

The views from the stylish rooms here are truly panoramic. Large windows face the Sumida River, the Tokyo Skytree observation tower, the wharves of Tokyo Bay, and Rainbow Bridge, which links the city to Odaiba Island (see pp34–5). There are several dining options, and a 20th-floor lounge bar offers amazing views of the bridge when it is illuminated after dark.

Shinjuku Prince Hotel

MAP B3 ■ 1-30-1 Kabukicho, Shinjuku-ku ■ 3205-1111 ■ www.princehotels.co.jp ■ ¥¥

Next to JR Shinjuku Station, this high-rise hotel offers incredible views of the Kabukicho entertainment zone from guest rooms and its 25th-floor restaurant. Good facilities and reasonably sized rooms.

Conrad Hotel

MAP M6 ■ 1-9-1 Higashi-Shinbashi, Minato-ku ■ 6388-8000 ■ www.conradtokyo.co.jp ■ ¥¥¥

The cityscape views and aerial perspectives of lush Hama Rikyu Garden (see p50) from this 37-story luxury hotel are unparalleled. Aromatic therapies, cedar wood spas, and superb cuisine will all contribute to a memorable stay.

Four Seasons Hotel Tokyo at Marunouchi

MAP N3 ■ Pacific Century Place, 1-11-1 Marunouchi, Chiyoda-ku ■ 5222-7222 ■ www.fourseasons.com/tokyo ■ ¥¥¥

Located close to Tokyo Station and the Imperial Palace (see pp12–13), this luxurious hotel has large rooms equipped with 3-D/Blu-ray built-in TVs, and offers great views of Central Tokyo. The service extended by the hotel's multilingual staff is impeccable.

For a key to hotel price categories see p128

Tokyo Station Hotel
MAP N3 ▪ 1-9-1 Marunouchi ▪ 5220-1111 ▪ www.thetokyostation hotel.jp ▪ ¥¥¥
Occupying one wing of the original 1914, red-brick Tokyo Station (see p76) building, this beautifully appointed hotel has been given a recent update. You can watch the *shinkansen* trains pull in and out of the station or gaze out at the bright towers of Marunouchi and Ginza.

The Westin Tokyo
MAP C2 ▪ 1-4-1 Mita, Meguro-ku ▪ 5423-7000 ▪ www.westin-tokyo.co.jp ▪ ¥¥¥
Styled along the lines of grand European hotels, the Westin stands just beyond the Ebisu Garden Place complex. Views from the middle and upper rooms toward the bay and inward over the city are stunning.

Ryokan and Minsuku

Andon Ryokan
MAP H1 ▪ 2-34-10 Nihonzutsumi, Taito-ku ▪ 3873-8611 ▪ www. andon.co.jp ▪ ¥
Enjoy the owner's antique collection while taking in the compact design of this ultra-modern *ryokan*. Every room has Internet access, a TV, and a DVD player. All floors have showers. There is also a communal Jacuzzi. The staff speak English.

Homeikan Honkan
MAP E2 ▪ 5-10-5 Hongo, Bunkyo-ku ▪ 3811-1187 ▪ www.homeikan.com ▪ ¥
This atmospheric old wooden *ryokan* with a lovely Japanese garden is

a designated Important Cultural Property. The inn's location in Hongo, a traditional neighborhood, enhances its charm. Communal bath. Credit cards are not accepted.

Hotel Fukudaya
MAP C2 ▪ 4-5-9 Aobadai, Meguro-ku ▪ 3467-5833 ▪ www2.gol.com/users/ ryokan-fukudaya ▪ ¥
There's a set of samurai armor displayed in the lobby of this small family-run inn, which is within walking distance of both Shibuya and Naka-Meguro. Most of the rooms are traditional with futon beds and tatami-mat floors. Communal bathroom.

Kimi Ryokan
MAP C1 ▪ 2-36-8 Ikebukuro, Toshima-ku ▪ 3971-3766 ▪ www.kimi-ryokan.jp ▪ ¥
Popular with budget travelers, this inn offers small but immaculate Japanese rooms. Bathing is communal. The place offers great value, so it is advisable to book ahead.

Ryokan Katsutaro
MAP F1 ▪ 4-16-8 Ikenohata, Taito-ku ▪ 3821-9808 ▪ www. katsutaro.com ▪ ¥
Seven Japanese-style rooms are provided at this friendly, family-run *ryokan* in a quiet, traditional district near Ueno Park (see pp20–21). It also has an annex in Yanaka.

Ryokan Sansuiso
MAP D2 ▪ 2-9-5 Higashi-Gotanda, Shinagawa-ku ▪ 3441-7475 ▪ www. sansuiso.net ▪ ¥
An affordable choice close to Gotanda Station. Some of the Japanese rooms

have baths, others have communal facilities. Note that there is a midnight curfew and credit cards are not accepted.

Ryokan Shigetsu
MAP R3 ▪ 1-31-11 Asakusa, Taito-ku ▪ 3843-2345 ▪ www.shigetsu. com ▪ ¥
This beautifully maintained *ryokan* is adorned with paper screen windows and tatami screen mats. The two traditional baths here are a highlight, with views respectively of Senso-ji temple and the city itself.

Sawanoya Ryokan
MAP F1 ▪ 2-3-11 Yanaka, Taito-ku ▪ 3822-2251 ▪ www.sawanoya.com ▪ ¥
A great place to meet fellow travelers, this long-established *ryokan* is popular with foreign guests. Rooms are small, but comfortable. There is a communal tub for guests, although some rooms do have en suite baths. Situated in the interesting old quarter of Yanaka, close to Ueno Park (see p20–21). Credit cards are not accepted.

Sukeroku no Yado Sadachiyo
MAP R2 ▪ 2-20-1 Asakusa, Taito-ku ▪ 3842-6431 ▪ www.sadachiyo.co.jp ▪ ¥
A sophisticated, modern Japanese inn located in a peaceful spot just a five-minute walk from Senso-ji temple (see pp14-15). Japanese-style rooms, which come in different sizes, allow you to fully immerse yourself in the Edo-period atmosphere. The staff are helpful, but not very fluent in English. Excellent communal Japanese bath.

Tokyo Ryokan

MAP Q3 ▪ 2-4-8 Nishi-Asakusa, Taito-ku ▪ 090-8879-3599 ▪ www.tokyoryokan.com ▪ ¥
Ideal for exploring Asakusa, this charming traditional place has communal bathing. No meals are provided, but there are many restaurants nearby.

Further Afield

Annex Turtle Hotori-an

MAP B1 ▪ 8-28 Takumicho, Nikko ▪ 0288-53-3663 ▪ www.turtle-nikko.com ▪ ¥
This business with English-speaking staff has been welcoming travelers to Nikko for decades. This is the more modern annex to their original guesthouse and has both Western and Japanese style rooms.

Fuji Hakone Guest House

MAP A2 ▪ 912 Sengokuhara, Hakone ▪ 0460-84-6577 ▪ www.fujihakone.com/en ▪ ¥
The English-speaking family who run this traditional-style inn are very welcoming and very knowledgeable about the area's attractions. Sleep on a futon and soak in an outdoor *onsen* bath.

Hotel New Grand

MAP B2 ▪ 10 Yamashita-cho, Naka-ku, Yokohama ▪ 045-681-1841 ▪ www.hotel-newgrand.co.jp ▪ ¥
A historic hotel in Japan's second-largest city, the Grand has a prime spot opposite a waterfront park and the contemporary cruise terminal. The public areas of the original building live up to their grand billing.

Hotel New Kamakura

MAP B2 ▪ 13-2 Onarimachi, Kamakura ▪ 0467-22-2230 ▪ www.newkamakura.com ▪ ¥
Close by the station, the New Kamakura is actually one of the temple town's oldest Western-style hotels with plenty of retro charm. Rooms, both Western and Japanese style, are split across two small buildings.

Nine Hours Narita Airport

MAP B2 ▪ Narita International Airport Terminal 2, 1-1 Furugome, Narita ▪ 0476-33-5109 ▪ www.ninehours.co.jp/en/narita ▪ ¥
Handy both for Tokyo's main international airport and as an affordable base for the attractions of Narita. Guests sleep in a roomy, state-of-the-art capsule. Luggage lockers and communal shower facilities for men and women are available.

Fuji Lake Hotel

MAP A2 ▪ 1 Funatsu, Fuji-Kawaguchiko-machi ▪ 0555-72-2209 ▪ www.fujilake.co.jp ▪ ¥¥
Stunningly located on the clear shores of Lake Kawaguchi with Mount Fuji as its backdrop, this 1930s hotel has bags of retro appeal. There is a sauna and Jacuzzi in the communal *onsen* bathroom and a viewing terrace if your room doesn't face Mount Fuji.

Fujiya Hotel

MAP B2 ▪ 359 Miyanoshita, Hakone ▪ 0460-82-2211 ▪ www.fujiyahotel.jp ▪ ¥¥
One of the oldest Western hotels in Japan and a true classic, the Fujiya has been in business since 1878, and the wonderful old building has drawn countless dignitaries and celebrities from around the world, including John Lennon. The main dining room is simply majestic. All rooms have a bath fed by natural hot springs.

Nikko Kanaya Hotel

MAP B1 ▪ 1300 Kami-Hatsuishi-machi, Nikko ▪ 0288-54-0001 ▪ www.kanayahotel.co.jp ▪ ¥¥
Built in 1873, this classic resort hotel presents an impressive blend of old-world charm and flawless service. Well-appointed rooms date from the Meiji era to the 1950s.

Yokohama Royal Park Hotel

MAP B2 ▪ 2-2-1-3 Minato Mirai, Nishi-ku, Yokohama ▪ 045-221-1111 ▪ www.yrph.com ▪ ¥¥
This hotel is ideal for those looking for great views. Rooms are located on the 52nd to 67th floors of the soaring Landmark Tower, offering a splendid vista of the waterfront and Mount Fuji.

Hoshinoya Fuji

MAP A2 ▪ 1408 Oishi, Fuji-Kawaguchiko-machi ▪ 050-3786-1144 ▪ www.hoshinoyafuji.com/en ▪ ¥¥¥
Japan's first glamping resort, Hoshinoya Fuji is as far from camping as you could imagine. Stay in stylish, minimalist cabins, eat under the stars and take part in a range of activities around the lake and Mount Fuji.

General Index

Acknowledgments

Author
Stephen Mansfield

Additional Contributor
Simon Richmond

Publishing Director Georgina Dee

Publisher Vivien Antwi

Design Director Phil Ormerod

Editorial Sophie Adam, Michelle Crane, Alice Fewery, Rachel Fox, Sally Schafer, Jackie Staddon

Design Cover Bess Daly, Maxine Pedliham

Design Hansa Babra, Tessa Bindloss, Richard Czapnik, Rahul Kumar, Bhavika Mathur, Marisa Renzullo, Stuti Tiwari, Vinita Venugopal

Picture Research Sumita Khatwani, Ellen Root, Lucy Sienkowska, Rituraj Singh

Cartography Dominic Beddow, Simonetta Giori, Casper Morris, Reetu Pandey

DTP Jason Little

Production Nancy-Jane Maun

Factchecker Bill Willis

Proofreader Leena Lane

Indexer Hilary Bird

First edition created by Quadrum Solutions, Mumbai

Revisions Team Bharti Karakoti, Sumita Khatwani, Shikha Kulkarni, Farah Sheikh, Tanveer Zaidi

Picture Credits

The publisher would like to thank the following for their kind permission to reproduce their photographs:
Key: a-above; b-below/bottom; c-centre; f-far; l-left; r-right; t-top

123RF.com: Kriengkrai Choochote 112tl; coward_lion 21c; Ivan Marchuk 74tl; sean pavone 20-1c, 106cl; Norikazu Satomi 10clb; yyäma3270 16bl.

3331 Arts Chiyoda: Chiyoda Arts Festival 2011 47cr.

Alamy Stock Photo: A.F. Archive 59br; AFLO/Nippon News/Natsuki Sakai 71cla; Aflo Co. Ltd 71bc, /Keiki Haginoya 31br; age fotostock/Javier Larrea 42b; Mark Bassett 4cr, 54b; Patrick Batchelder 3tl, 72-3; Paul Brown 92-3; DEA/G. Sosio 34br; Songquan Deng 15bl; World Discovery 32cl, 4tr, 67tr, 67cl, 78cla, 104clb; EDU Vision 52tl, 76br; F1online digitale Bildagentur GmbH /S. Tauqueur 11br; Gavin Hellier 69cl; hemis.fr/Patrick Frilet 54cla; Peter Horree 24cr, 69tr; Alex Hunter 51tl; INTERFOTO/Fine Arts 45tl, /History 38br; Japan Stock Photography 77tl; Japan travel

photography 66br; JTB MEDIA CREATION, Inc /JTB Photo/UIG 11cla, 40cl, 96t; Andrey Kekyalyaynen 14clb; John Lander 28br, 29tl; Yannick Luthy 114bl; Oleksiy Maksymenko 49b, 55tr; Greg McNevin 53cl; Trevor Mogg 56t; Luciano Mortula 43cr; Motion/Horizon Images 70tl; James Nesterwitz 32br; Sean Pavone, 17tl, 34-5, 57clb, 68cla, 103tl; PersimmonPictures.com 52b; Phanie/Voisin 57tr; Prisma Bildagentur AG/Raga Jose Fuste 13cr, 56br; Alex Segre 66tl; John Steele 94tl; Jeremy Sutton-Hibbert 53tr, 63b; Ivan Vdovin 27ca; Steve Vidler 88tl; Peter M. Wilson 11cr; Masayuki Yamashita 50cl.

Asakusa Imahan: 62t.

AWL Images: Christian Kober 117cra; Travel Pix Collection 1, 2tl, 4t, 8-9.

Blue Note Tokyo: 61t.

Bridgeman Images: Seiji Togo Memorial Sompo Japan Nipponkoa Museum of Art, Tokyo, Japan *Sunflowers* (1889) by Vincent van Gogh 108tr; Werner Forman Archive 80tl.

Conrad Tokyo: TwentyEight 65b.

Corbis: 39br; All Canada Photos/Ken Paul 15cr; Atlantide Phototravel /Massimo Borchi 12br, 75t, 82-3, 111bl; Bettmann 39cl; Tibor Bognar 86r; incamerastock /Iain Masterton, 95cra; Masterfile /F. Lukasseck 96br; Nippon News/AFLO 102cl; Nippon News /AFLO /Rory Merry 110cl; Photononstop /Calle Montes 109cl.

Design Festa: 70cr.

Dreamstime.com: Andreevaee 89cl; Bennnn 115cla; Bennymarty 50bl, 71tr; Ratchadaporn Chullanan 30cla; Cowardlion 20br, 41tl, 76tl, 86cl, 97cl, 102b, 113t; dragoncello 31tl; Foto99 95b; Fotokon 46bl; Gjeerawut 87tr; Hiro1775 49tl, 114cl; Javarman 107b; Mihai-bogdan Lazar 6cla; Esteban Miyahira 113br; Mnsanthoshkumar 79bl; Luciano Mortula 7cra, 14-5; Sean Pavone 10cla, 40b, 82tl; Jaturun Phuengphut_tharak 4cla; Ppy2010ha 105ca; Mohd Fuad Salleh 10crb; Siraanamwong 100cla; Torsakarin 51bl; Maria Vazquez 88b; Sarah Wilkie 5clb; Buddhapong Wongsanont 10c; Xiye 31clb; Yuryz 55clb, 68b.

Getty Images: AFP/Reuters/Issei Kato 59cla, /Toshifumi Kitamura 58tl; Aro @ Photography 15crb; Marco Brivio 12-3; Print Collector 38cla; JTB Photo 17crb; Koichi Kamoshida 58crb; LightRocket/John S Lander 27b, 28cla; Sergio Lora 11crb, 32-3; takau99 29crb; UIG/JTB Photo 16-7, 101t.

Goodbeer Faucets: 65t.

iStockphoto.com: helovi 35crb; Hiro1775 116b; magicflute002 2tr, 14cla, 36-7b;

MiriamPolito 42cla; orpheus26 30-1; Marek Slusarczyk 10b; shirophoto 4b; Thananat 21tl; TwilightShow 3tr, 118-9; winhorse 81b.

Las Chicas: 105crb.

Mori Art Musem: 45b.

National Film Center Exhibition: 81tr.

National Museum of Emerging Science and Innovation: 35tr.

The National Museum of Modern Art, Tokyo: 75br; *Mother and Child* (1934) by Uemura Shoen, color on silk, framed, 168.0 × 115.5 cm, Important Cultural Property 12cl.

NTT InterCommunication Center: 108bl.

Park Hyatt Tokyo: 64cl,111tr.

Photoshot: 90t.

Pink Cow: 98b.

Robert Harding Picture Library: Tibor Bognar 94cra; Lucas Vallecillos 4crb, 104tr.

SuperStock: Steve Vidler 22-3.

Tokyo Metropolitan Edo-Tokyo Museum: 18-9, 19cb.

Images courtesy of Tokyo National Museum: 11tl, 24bl, 25tl, 25bc, 25clb, 26t, 26clb, 45c.

Womb: 60br

Cover
Front and spine: **Dreamstime.com:** Tomas1111.

Back: **Dreamstime.com:** F11photo tr, Natalia Lisovskaya crb, Tomas1111 bc, Nathapon Triratanachat tl; **iStockphoto.com:** TommL cla.

Pull Out Map Cover
Dreamstime.com: Tomas1111.

All other images © Dorling Kindersley
For further information see:
www.dkimages.com

As a guide to abbreviations in visitor information blocks: **Adm** = admission charge

Penguin
Random
House

Printed and bound in China

First American Edition 2009

Published in the United States by:
DK Publishing, 345 Hudson Street,
New York, New York 10014

Published in Great Britain in 2009
by Dorling Kindersley Limited
80 Strand, London WC2R 0RL

Copyright © 2009, 2019 Dorling
Kindersley Limited

A Penguin Random House Company

18 19 20 21 10 9 8 7 6 5 4 3 2 1

Reprinted with revisions 2011, 2013, 2015, 2017, 2019

A catalog record for this book is available from the Library of Congress.

A CIP catalogue record is available from the British Library.

ISSN 1479-344X

ISBN 978-0-2413-6466-6

SPECIAL EDITIONS OF DK TRAVEL GUIDES

DK Travel Guides can be purchased in bulk quantities at discounted prices for use in promotions or as premiums. We also offer special editions and personalized jackets, corporate imprints, and excerpts from all of our books, tailored specifically to meet your own needs.

To find out more, please contact:

in the US
specialsales@dk.com
in the UK
travelguides@uk.dk.com
in Canada
specialmarkets@dk.com
in Australia
**penguincorporatesales@
penguinrandomhouse.com.au**

MIX
Paper from
responsible sources
FSC™ C018179
www.fsc.org

Phrase Book

The origins of the Japanese language are unclear. Written Japanese uses a combination of four scripts: Chinese ideograms, known as *kanji*; two syllable-based alphabet systems known as *hiragana* and *katakana*; and the Latin alphabet, *romaji*. *Hiragana* and *katakana* are similar, *katakana* often functioning in a similar way to the use of italics in English. Traditionally, Japanese is written in vertical columns from top right to bottom left, though the Western system is widely used. There are several romanization systems: the Hepburn system is used in this guide. To simplify romanization, macrons (long marks over vowels to indicate longer pronunciation) have not been used. Japanese pronunciation is fairly straightforward, and many words are "Japanized" versions of Western words. This Phrase Book gives the English word or phrase, followed by the Japanese script, then the romanization, adapted to aid pronunciation.

Guidelines for Pronunciation

When reading the romanization, give the same emphasis to all syllables. The practice in English of giving one syllable greater stress may render a Japanese word incomprehensible.

Pronounce vowels as in these English words:

a	as the "a" in "again"
e	as in "red"
i	as in "in"
o	as in "solid"
u	as the "u" in "cuckoo"

When two vowels are used together, sound each letter separately:

ai	as in "pine"
ae	as if written "ah-eh"
ei	as in "pay"

Consonants are pronounced as in English. The letter *g* is always hard as in "gate," and *j* is always soft as in "joke." *R* is pronounced something between *r* and *l*. *F* is sometimes pronounced as *h*. "Si" always becomes "shi," but some people pronounce "shi" as "hi." *V* in Western words (e.g., "video") becomes *b*. If followed by a consonant, *n* may be pronounced as either *n* or *m*.

All consonants except *n* are always either followed by a vowel or doubled; however, sometimes an *i* or *u* is barely pronounced. In this Phrase Book, to aid pronunciation, apostrophes are used where an *i* or *u* is barely pronounced within a word, and double consonants where this occurs at the end of a word.

Dialects

Standard Japanese is used and understood throughout Japan by people of all backgrounds. But on a colloquial level, there are significant differences in both pronunciation and vocabulary, even between the Tokyo and Osaka-Kyoto areas, and rural accents are very strong.

Polite Words and Phrases

There are several different levels of politeness in the Japanese language, according to status, age, and situation. In everyday conversation, politeness levels are simply a question of the length of verb endings (longer is more polite), but in formal conversation entirely different words (*keigo*) are used. The level given in this Phrase Book is neutral, yet polite.

In an Emergency

Help!	たすけて！	Tas'kete!
Stop!	とめて！	Tomete!
Call a doctor!	医者をよんで ください！	Isha o yonde kudasai!
Call an ambulance!	救急車を よんでください！	Kyukyusha o yonde kudasai!
Call the police!	警察を よんでください！	Keisatsu o yonde kudasai!
Fire!	火事！	Kaji!
Where is the hospital?	病院はどこに ありますか？	Byoin wa doko ni arimass-ka?
police box	交番	koban

Communication Essentials

Yes/no.	はい／いいえ	Hai/ie.
Thank you.	ありがとう。	Arigato.
Please (offering).	どうぞ。	Dozo.
Please (asking).	おねがいします。	Onegai shimass.
Do you speak English?	英語が 話せますか？	Eigo o hanasemass-ka?
I can't speak Japanese.	日本語は 話せません。	Nihongo wa hanasemasen.
Sorry/Excuse me!	すみません。	Sumimasen!
Could you help me please? (not emergency)	ちょっと手伝って いただけません か？	Chotto tets'datte itadakemasen-ka?

Useful Phrases

My name is…	わたしの 名前は・・	Watashi no namae wa… dess.
How do you do, pleased to meet you.	はじめまして、 どうぞ よろしく。	Hajime-mash'te dozo yorosh'ku.
How are you?	お元気ですか？	Ogenki dess-ka?
Good morning.	おはよう ございます。	Ohayo gozaimass.
Good afternoon. good day.	こんにちは。	Konnichiwa.
Good evening.	こんばんは。	Konbanwa.
Good night.	おやすみなさい。	Oyasumi nasai.
Good-bye.	さよなら。	Sayonara.
What is (this)?	（これは）何 ですか？	(Kore wa) nan dess-ka?
Where can I get …?	・・・はどこに ・・・？	…wa doko ni arimass-ka?
How much is it?	いくらですか？	Ikura dess-ka?
What time is …?	何時ですか？	…nan-ji dess-ka?
Cheers! (toast)	乾杯！	Kanpai!
Where is the restroom/toilet?	お手洗い／おトイレ はどこ ですか？	Toire wa doko dess-ka?
Here's my business card.	名刺をどうぞ。	Meishi o dozo.
How do you use this?	これをどうやって 使いますか？	Kore o doyatte ts'kaimass-ka?

Useful Words

I	わたし	watashi
woman	女性	josei
man	男性	dansei
wife	奥さん	ok'san
husband	主人	shujin
big/small	大きい／小さい	ookii/chiisai
hot/cold	暑い／寒い	atsui/samui
warm	温かい	atatakai
good/ not good/bad	いい／よくない／ 悪い	ii/yokunai/warui
free (no charge)	ただ／無料	tada/muryo
here	ここ	koko
there	あそこ	asoko
this	これ	kore

that (nearby)	それ	sore
that (far away)	あれ	are
what?	何?	nani?
when?	いつ?	itsu?
why?	なぜ?/どうして?	naze?/dosh'te?
where?	どこ?	doko?
who?	誰?	dare?
which way?	どちら?	dochira?
enough	じゅうぶん/結構	jubun/kekko

Signs

open	営業中	eigyo-chu
closed	休日	kyujitsu
entrance	入口	iriguchi
exit	出口	deguchi
danger	危険	kiken
emergency exit	非常口	hijo-guchi
information	案内	annai
restroom, toilet	お手洗い/手洗い/おトイレ/トイレ	otearai/tearai/otoire/toire
free (vacant)	空き	aki
men	男	otoko
women	女	onna

Money

Could you change this into yen please.	これを円に替えてください。	Kore o en ni kaete kudasai.
I'd like to cash these travelers' checks.	このトラベラーズチェックを現金にしたいです。	Kono toraberazu chekku o genkin ni shitai dess.
Do you take credit cards/travelers' checks?	クレジットカード/トラベラーズチェックで払えますか?	Kurejitto kado/toraberazu chekku de haraemass-ka?
bank	銀行	ginko
cash	現金	genkin
credit card	クレジットカード	kurejitto kado
currency exchange office	両替所	ryogaejo
dollars	ドル	doru
pounds	ポンド	pondo
yen	円	en

Keeping in Touch

Where is a telephone?	電話はどこにありますか	Denwa wa doko ni arimass-ka?
May I use your phone?	電話を使ってもいいですか	Denwa o ts'katte mo ii dess-ka?
Hello, this is	もしもし、…です。	Moshi-moshi, … dess.
I'd like to make an international call.	国際電話、お願いします	Kokusai denwa, onegai shimass.
airmail	航空便	kokubin
email	メール	me-ru
fax	ファクス	fak'su
postcard	ハガキ	hagaki
post office	郵便局	yubin-kyoku
stamp	切手	kitte
telephone booth	公衆電話	koshu denwa
telephone card	テレフォンカード	terefon kado

Staying in a Hotel

Do you have any vacancies?	部屋がありますか?	Heya ga arimass-ka?
I have a reservation.	予約をしてあります。	Yoyaku o sh'te arimass.
I'd like a room with a bathroom.	お風呂つきの部屋、お願いします。	Ofuro-ts'ki no heya, onegai shimass.
What is the charge per night?	一泊いくらですか?	Ippaku ikura dess-ka?

Japanese-style inn	旅館	ryokan
Japanese-style room	和室	wa-shitsu
key	鍵	kagi
front desk	フロント	furonto
single/twin room	シングル/ツイ	shinguru/tsuin
shower	シャワー	shawa
Western-style hotel	ホテル	hoteru
Western-style room	洋室	yo-shitsu
Is tax included in the price?	税込みですか?	Zeikomi dess-ka?
Can I leave my luggage here for a little while?	荷物をちょっとここに預けてもいいですか?	Nimotsu o chotto koko ni azukete mo ii dess-ka?
air-conditioning	冷房/エアコン	reibo/eakon
bath	お風呂	ofuro
check-out	チェックアウト	chekku-auto

Eating Out

A table for one/two/three, please.	一人/二人/三人、お願いします。	Hitori/futari/sannin, onegai shimass.
May I see the menu.	メニュー、お願いします。	Menyu, onegai shimass.
Is there a set menu?	定食がありますか?	Teishoku ga arimass-ka?
I'd like	私は…がいいです。	Watashi wa … ga ii dess.
May I have one of those?	それをひとつ、お願いします。	Sore o hitotsu, onegai shimass.
I am a vegetarian.	私はベジタリアンです。	Watashi wa bejitarian dess.
Waiter/waitress!	ちょっとすみません。	Chotto sumimasen!
What would you recommend?	おすすめは何ですか?	Osusume wa nan dess-ka?
How do you eat this?	これはどうやって食べますか?	Kore wa doyatte tabemass-ka?
May we have the check please.	お勘定、お願いします。	Okanjo, onegai shimass.
May we have some more ...	もっと…、お願いします。	Motto …, onegai shimass.
The meal was very good, thank you.	ごちそうさまでした。おいしかったです。	Gochiso-sama desh'ta, oishikatta dess.
assortment	盛り合わせ	moriawase
boxed meal	弁当	bento
breakfast	朝食	cho-shoku
buffet	バイキング	baikingu
delicious	おいしい	oishii
dinner	夕食	yu-shoku
to drink	飲む	nomu
a drink	飲みもの	nomimono
to eat	食べる	taberu
food	食べもの/ごはん	tabemono/gohan
full (stomach)	おなかがいっぱい	onaka ga ippai
hot/cold	熱い/冷たい	atsui/tsumetai
hungry	おなかがすいた	onaka ga suita
Japanese food	和食	wa-shoku
lunch	昼食	chu-shoku
set menu	セット/定食	setto (snack)/teishoku (meal)
spicy	辛い	karai
sweet, mild	甘い	amai
Western food	洋食	yo-shoku
pepper	こしょう	kosho
salt	塩	shio
vegetables	野菜	yasai
sugar	砂糖	sato

Places to Eat

Cafeteria/canteen	食堂	shokudo
Chinese restaurant	中華料理屋	chuka-ryori-ya
coffee shop	喫茶店	kissaten
local bar	飲み屋／居酒屋	nomiya/izakaya
ramen stall	ラーメン屋	ramen-ya
restaurant	レストラン／料理屋	resutoran/ryori-ya
sushi on a conveyor belt	回転寿司	kaiten-zushi
upscale restaurant	料亭	ryotei
upscale vegetarian restaurant	精進料理屋	shojin-ryori-ya

Menu Decoder

ビール	biiru	beer
ホットコーヒー	hotto-kohi	coffee (hot)
お茶	ocha	green tea
アイスコーヒー	aisu-kohi	iced coffee: black
カフェオレ	kafe-o-re	café au lait
レモンティー	remon ti	lemon tea
ミルク／牛乳	miruku/gyunyu	milk
ミネラルウォーター	mineraru uota	mineral water
酒	sake	rice wine
（甘酒）	(ama-zake)	rice wine (non-alcoholic)
紅茶	kocha	tea (Western-style)
ミルクティー	miruku ti	tea with milk
水	mizu	water
ウイスキー	uis'ki	whiskey
たけのこ	takenoko	bamboo shoots
とうふ	tofu	beancurd
もやし	moyashi	bean sprouts
豆	mame	beans
ビーフ／牛肉	bifu/gyuniku	beef
ふぐ	fugu	blowfish
かつお／ツナ	katsuo/tsuna	bonito, tuna
とり／鶏肉	tori/toriniku	chicken
かに	kani	crab
あひる	ahiru	duck
うなぎ	unagi	eel
たまご	tamago	egg
なす	nasu	eggplant/aubergine
みそ	miso	fermented soybean paste
納豆	natto	fermented soybeans
さしみ	sashimi	fish (raw)
油揚げ	abura-age	fried tofu
くだもの	kudamono	fruit
会席	kaiseki	haute cuisine
ニシン	nishin	herring
アイスクリーム	aisu-kurimu	ice cream
伊勢えび	ise-ebi	lobster
さば	saba	mackerel
肉	niku	meat
そば	soba	buckwheat noodles
ラーメン	ramen	ramen noodles
うどん	udon	thick wheat noodles
そうめん	somen	thin wheat noodles
たこ	tako	octopus
カキ	kaki	oyster, persimmon
つけもの	ts'kemono	pickles
豚肉	butaniku	pork
ごはん	gohan	cooked rice
米	kome	uncooked rice
サラダ	sarada	salad
鮭	sake	salmon
ソーセージ	soseji	sausage
えび	ebi	shrimp
いか	ika	squid
鱒	masu	trout
ウニ	uni	sea urchin
すいか	suika	watermelon
ぼたん／いのしし	botan/inoshishi	wild boar
汁／スープ	shiru/supu	soup
しょうゆ	shoyu	soy sauce
スパゲティ	supageti	spaghetti
五目寿司	gomoku-zushi	sushi (mixed)

Numbers

0	ゼロ	zero
1	一	ichi
2	二	ni
3	三	san
4	四	yon/shi
5	五	go
6	六	roku
7	七	nana/shichi
8	八	hachi
9	九	kyu
10	十	ju
11	十一	ju-ichi
12	十二	ju-ni
20	二十	ni-ju
21	二十一	ni-ju-ichi
22	二十二	ni-ju-ni
30	三十	san-ju
40	四十	yon-ju
100	百	hyaku
101	百一	hyaku-ichi
200	二百	ni-hyaku
300	三百	san-byaku
400	四百	yon-hyaku
500	五百	go-hyaku
600	六百	ro-ppyaku
700	七百	nana-hyaku
800	八百	ha-ppyaku
900	九百	kyu-hyaku
1,000	千	sen
1,001	千一	sen-ichi
2,000	二千	ni-sen
10,000	一万	ichi-man
20,000	二万	ni-man
100,000	十万	ju-man
1,000,000	百万	hyaku-man

Time

Monday	月曜日	getsu-yobi
Tuesday	火曜日	ka-yobi
Wednesday	水曜日	sui-yobi
Thursday	木曜日	moku-yobi
Friday	金曜日	kin-yobi
Saturday	土曜日	do-yobi
Sunday	日曜日	nichi-yobi
minute	分	pun/fun
this year	今年	kotoshi
last year	去年	kyonen
next year	来年	rainen
one year	一年	ichi-nen
late	遅い	osoi
early	早い	hayai
soon	すぐ	sugu

Tokyo Street Index

Tokyo Areas Index